An
Exact
Likeness

The Portraits of John Wesley

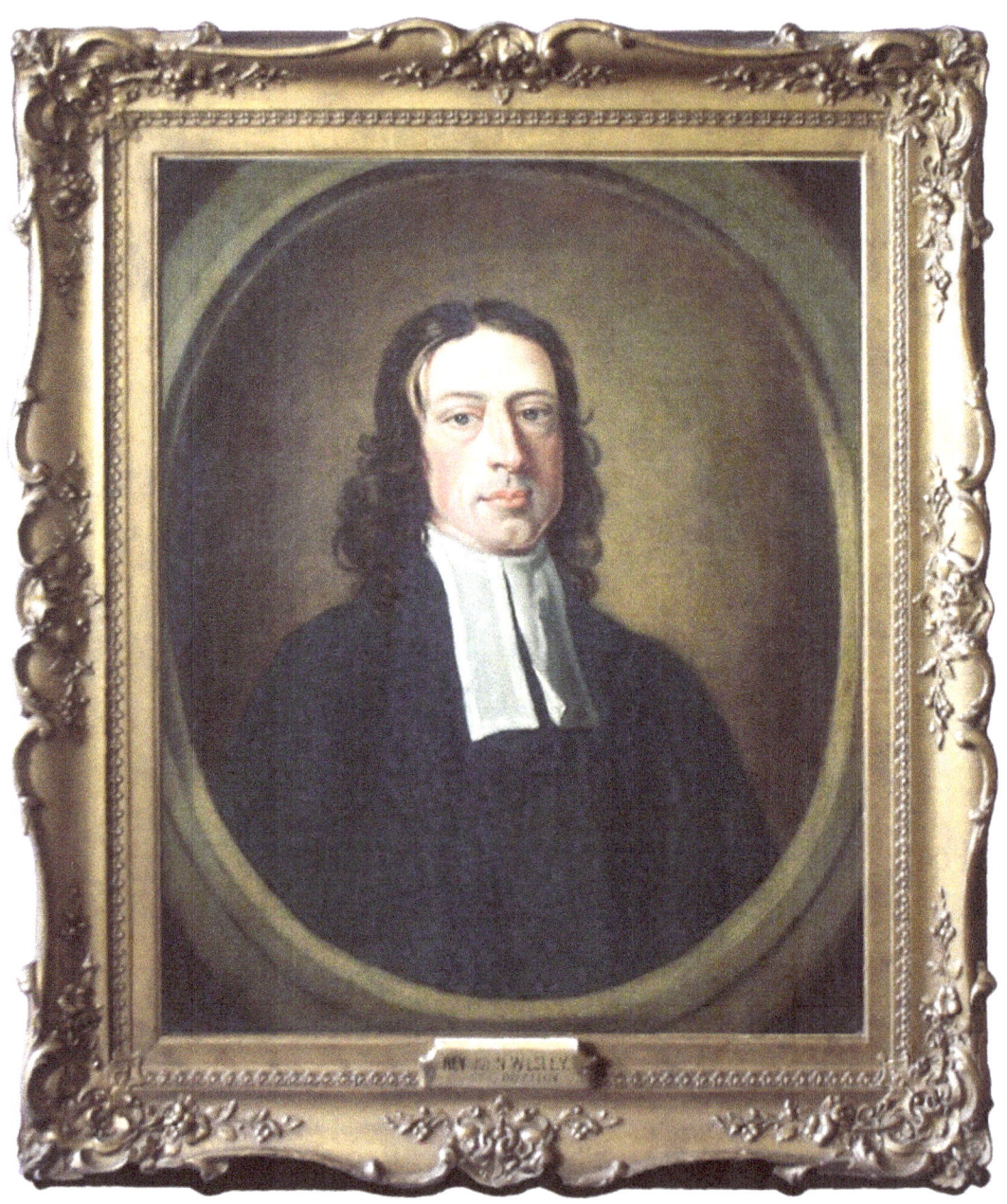

John Wesley, by William Harley (c. 1745) after John Michael Williams, oil painting

An
Exact
Likeness

The Portraits
of John Wesley

Richard P. Heitzenrater

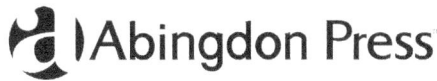
Abingdon Press

Nashville

AN EXACT LIKENESS:
PORTRAITS OF JOHN WESLEY

Copyright © 2016 by Richard P. Heitzenrater

Library of Congress Cataloging-in-Publication Data has been requested.

ISBN 978-1-5018-1660-4

16 17 18 19 20 21 22 23 24 25—10 9 8 7 6 5 4 3 2 1
MANUFACTURED IN THE UNITED STATES OF AMERICA

To my wife,
Karen

Contents

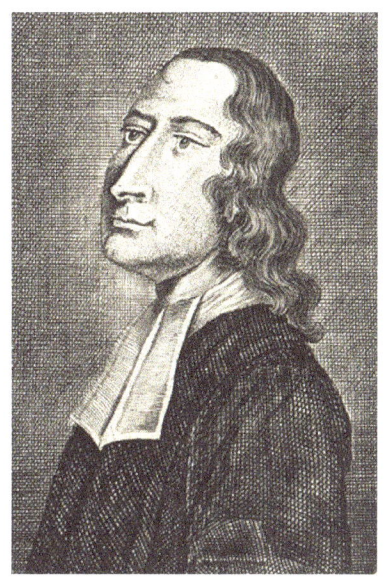

Introduction

$\mathbf{\mathit{F}}$aces are more than a montage of organs that see, breathe, speak, hear, eat, sing, smell, and yell. As Josephine Tey points out in her mystery novel *The Daughter of Time,* the slant of an eyebrow, the set of a mouth, the look of the eye, the firmness of a chin, often can provide evidence of character that is as telling as a report card or a police blotter. And those features depicted on portraits of individuals can be equally telling of the person's inner nature or perhaps of what the artist thinks (or wants the viewer to think) about the person being portrayed. Sometimes a portrait might be even more useful than a biography: "The real history is written in forms not meant as history."[1]

Portraits are many times viewed as successful or not because of the perception by the public of the person's significance or character, rather than for the value of the portrait as a work of art or the reproduction of the person's photographic likeness.[2] The image portrays something of the person's soul or personality.

---

1. Josephine Tey, *The Daughter of Time* (New York: Collier Books, 1988), 90. In graduate classes on the Reformation being taught at Duke University, Prof. Hans Hillerbrand liked to claim that the portraits of Charles V, and especially the shiftiness evident in his eyes, said more about his devious nature than any biography could have portrayed.

2. See Marcia Pointon, *Hanging the Head: Portraiture and Social Formation in Eighteenth-Century England* (New Haven: Yale University Press, 1993), 41.

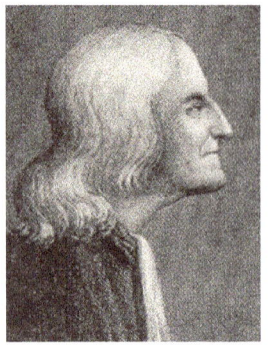 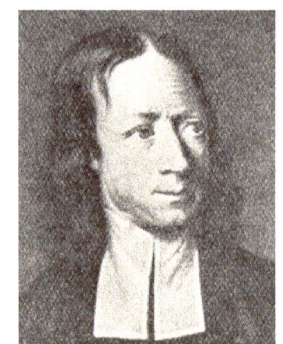 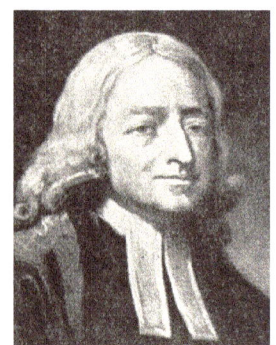

The title of this work, *"An Exact Likeness,"* appears here in quotation marks for two reasons: (1) Wesley himself used this type of phrase to describe many of the portraits of him that were produced during his lifetime, even though they were unlike his appearance or each other; and (2) there is an irony inherent therein, since the portraits differ greatly and produce no consensus as to his actual likeness.

As for the portraits, Wesley's comments about them were equally blunt at times and evasive at others. He did not completely avoid sitting for artists, though he tended to live out Samuel Johnson's view of him as always being in a hurry. He had little time or money for what he considered frivolities, even though the practice of portrait painting was becoming a more familiar feature of the British scene as the century progressed. And scholars are beginning to see and appreciate this development in the eighteenth century, when portraiture was becoming more common among the non-royal, non-governmental leaders. Portrait painting became one of the more obvious and perhaps practical implementations of the growing Enlightenment view of the importance of the individual self across the cultural landscape.

On occasion, my students in the Wesley Studies seminar have been asked to read Josephine Tey's detective novel before the course began. Then on the first day, I would give each of them a different photocopy of a portrait, explaining that they were all pictures of eighteenth-century clergymen (see above,

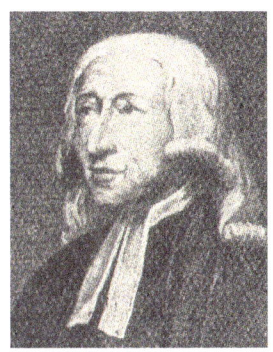 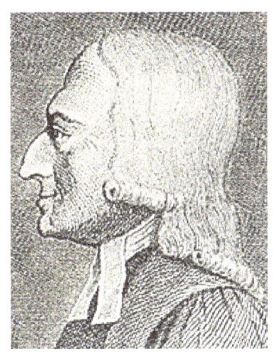 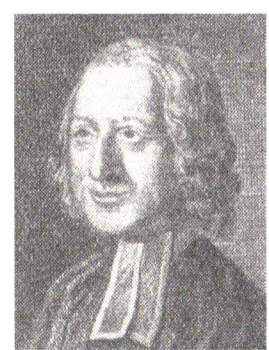

engravings of portraits by Worlidge, Hunter, Romney, Hamilton, Nasmyth, and anonymous). They were then asked to describe, as best they could, based on the picture, the character of the person as portrayed in their photocopy.

The descriptions of these "clergy" by the students were fascinatingly variant, as were the portraits they were examining. Sooner or later, one of the students would guess that perhaps the pictures were all purported to be of Wesley. Nevertheless, the descriptions that they had produced in the meantime were very revealing of their interpretations of the artists' intentions and perspectives, perhaps of the intended or hoped-for interpretations by the contemporary viewers, as well as their own interpretive slant on the eighteenth century. The variant portrayals and interpretations of Wesley's portraits often reflect the diverse interpretations of his writings, showing him in both cases to be a very elusive character, to both artists and writers, as well as to viewers and readers.

Contemporary references, including Wesley's own writings, seem to indicate that he allowed at least ten artists to spend time with him in their endeavor to create an artistic likeness: George Vertue, John Williams, John Russell, Nathaniel Hone, Johann Zoffany, Enoch Wood, George Romney, William Hamilton, Thomas Horsley, and Reginald Edward Arnold—seven of them painters. Six of these painters were notable artists of the day, indicated by their membership in the Royal Academy, and some of the others executed their craft well.

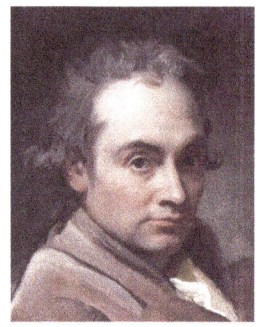 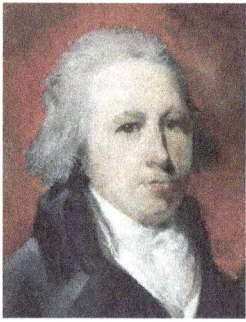 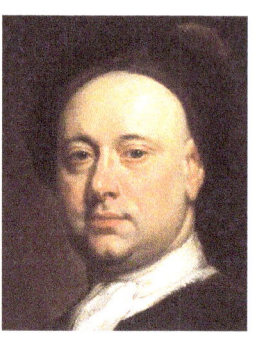 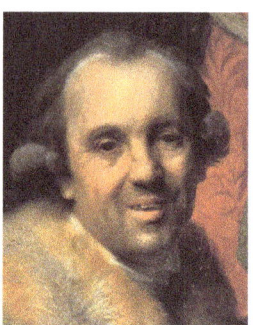

George Romney   **William Hamilton, R.A.**   **George Vertue**   **Johann Zoffany, R.A.**

Wesley seems never to have actually sat for Sir Joshua Reynolds, one of the founders of the Royal Academy, although it is frequently hypothesized that he did.

Wesley noted that some of the portrait painters took a relatively short time to finish their work, while he seems to cringe at the need of some others for taking more time, which he considered to be very valuable. After sitting for Enoch Wood to create a bust of him in 1781, Wesley began complaining of the amount of time he was wasting, upon which Wood noted that if the sitter would just look up from his book once or twice, it would not take nearly as long. After Wesley acquiesced on this point, he declared that the bust was a bit melancholy in the face. Wood apparently convinced Wesley to sit a bit longer, and after a short bit of reworking, Wesley himself said that Wood should not touch it again or risk damaging a fine piece of work.[3]

Some of the contemporary Wesley portraits reveal a great deal about Wesley, about the artists, and about the public of that time. Some misinformation associated with the portraits requires careful attention.[4]

In the examination of these portraits, four questions bear consideration when appropriate: (1) how are they similar or different; (2) what was Wesley's attitude toward the portrait,

3. John Kerslake, *Early Georgian Portraits* (London: Her Majesty's Stationery Office, 1977), 1:302-3.

4. With regard to the paintings and prints of Wesley, Kerslake commented thirty-five years ago, "A detailed critical survey of the portraiture is overdue." Ibid., 301. Very little has happened in the meantime to change that sentiment.

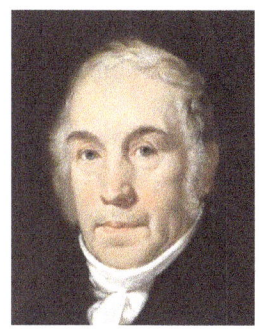 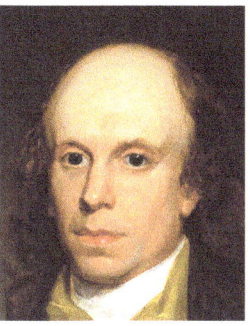 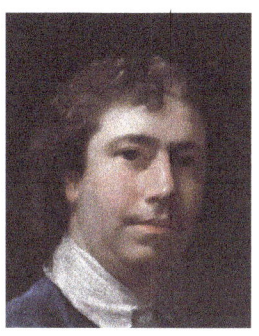 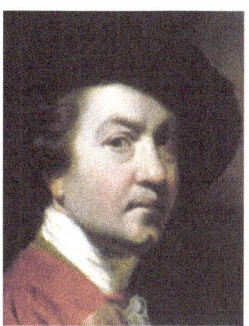

Enoch Wood   John Flaxman, R.A.   Nathaniel Hone, R.A.   Joshua Reynolds, R.A.

if any; (3) how did the public respond to these portrayals; and (4) what was the artist attempting to convey? This survey will focus on the main portraits and their derivatives, looking at them within the three main features of the Wesleyan *persona* that developed over the years: Oxford don, Methodist preacher, notable person. Although these types seemed to arise in chronological order, there is some overlap between categories, especially toward the end of Wesley's life and beyond.

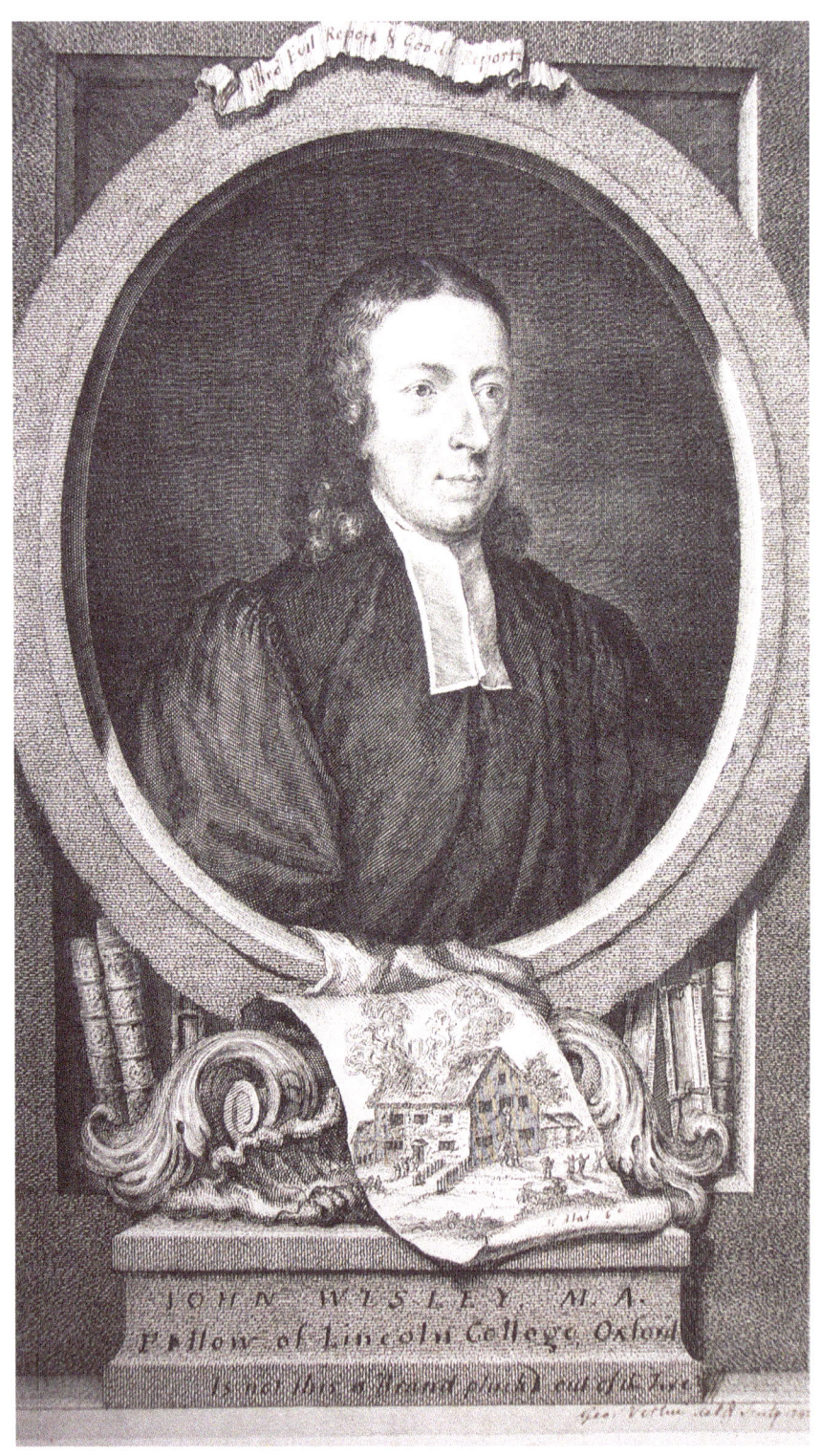

John Wesley, by George Vertue (drawn 1741; printed 1742)

Early Portraits of Wesley

*T*his survey of Wesley portraits starts with a brief mention of two etchings that precede the first painted portrait.[5]

Wesley's diary from the period mentions visiting the home of George Vertue, artist and engraver, in April, and then again on June 3 and 5, 1741.[6] These last two visits to Vertue, presumably in his studio, were for two or three hours in the morning, the time of day when many artists were hosting sitters for portraits. These visits seem to have resulted in an early engraved portrait of Wesley, a proof of which was dated by hand in pencil as by Vertue ("del. & sculpt.") in 1742 and probably published shortly thereafter.[7]

5. See facing page (state 1). Vertue also produced an earlier engraving in 1736: "Dr. Wesley sitting, *ad vivum* del GV," referring to his engraving of Samuel for the frontispiece of *Dissertations on Job*. Kerslake mentions over thirty portraits and prints, focusing on the three painted portraits in the National Portrait Gallery in London. Freeman M. O'Donoghue and Henry Mendelssohn Hake focus on the British Museum, London, providing a list of thirty portraits engraved during Wesley's lifetime or within two years of his death. Catalogue of *Engraved British Portraits in the Department of Prints and Drawings in the British Museum*, 5 vols. (London: British Museum, 1908–25), 4:439-41. We have included nearly a hundred portrayals of Wesley in this book, about eighty of them done between 1741 and 1791 (the year of his death).

6. April 11 in the early afternoon: "1.15 Walked; Short's Gardens; Vertue's, necessary talk. 2.30"; on Wednesday, June 5: "8.45 At Mr Vertue's. 11"; and on Friday, June 5: "9 At Mr Vertue's. 12." *Journal & Diaries II*, in *The Works of John Wesley* (Nashville: Abingdon, 1976—), 19:457, 463.

7. Horace Walpole (*Anecdotes of Painting in England, with Some Account of the Principal Artists* [London: Chatto and Windus, 1876], 3:276) mentions that there was a hiatus in Vertue's work for two years after the death of his friend Lord Oxford on June 16, 1741, which would mean that the Wesley sittings would have come just before that hiatus and the proof engraving would have come during that break, perhaps printed by another artist in Vertue's shop. Vertue's first published engraving of Wesley, using the Williams face, is dated 1745 (see below).

This engraving contains a ribbon on the top of the oval containing the portrait, saying "Thro' evil report and good report," and a small vignette at the bottom showing Wesley's escape from the Epworth fire in 1709, with the note, *"Anno Ætat 6°* [*sexto*—six]"—close to correct: he was actually in his sixth year, a few months from his sixth birthday. Below that is the quotation, "Is not this a brand pluck'd out of the fire?"— handwritten on the early proof but engraved on the later published editions.[8]

Samuel Badcock refers back to this vignette on an early portrait, in a reflection published in 1784, as proof that Wesley from an early stage had an image of himself as having been preserved by God for a special destiny, a charge that Wesley disputed in writing.[9] By 1742, Wesley had published a few minor items, including one installment of his journal, but was not a major figure on the British religious scene yet, certainly not as notorious as George Whitefield, who was the "Methodist" most frequently attacked in print in the early forties. So it is no surprise that no one had thought to do a portrait of Wesley up to this time.

The portrait of Wesley that is often said to be the earliest is somewhat primitive in form and technique. It has the head tilted slightly backward, giving Wesley a somewhat haughty appearance (easily interpreted as looking "down the nose" at the viewer), which might be the result of artist's instructions, or perhaps was a natural inclination of the Oxford don whom some people criticized as being somewhat aloof. But Peter Forsaith has made the credible suggestion that this portrait is what Wesley was describing in his comments about Downes in November 1774 after the latter's death.[10] At that point, Wesley noted that thirty years previous, John Downes was a young Methodist preacher who accompanied Wesley. One

---

8. This wording is a slight variation not only of the quotations from Amos and Zechariah (brand/firebrand, burning/fire), but also from some of the uses of the phrase by Wesley, which at times substituted "from" for "out of" and alternated between "fire" and "burning." Rarely does he ever cite correctly either biblical verse, but tends to conflate "Is not this a brand plucked out of the fire?" (Zech. 3:2) and "Ye were as a firebrand plucked out of the burning." (Amos 4:11).

9. See letters of 1784 in my *Elusive Mr. Wesley,* 2nd ed. (Nashville: Abingdon, 2003), 44–46.

10. Personal conversation at Manchester, England, in the summer of 2011.

day while shaving, the latter noticed Downes carving the head of a stick. When asked what he was doing, Downes said, "I am taking your face, which I intend to engrave on a copperplate." This early pose, then, could easily be seen as having the head tilted in a shaving position, thus connecting it with the comment of Downes, who then made the necessary tools and materials, engraved a copperplate, and

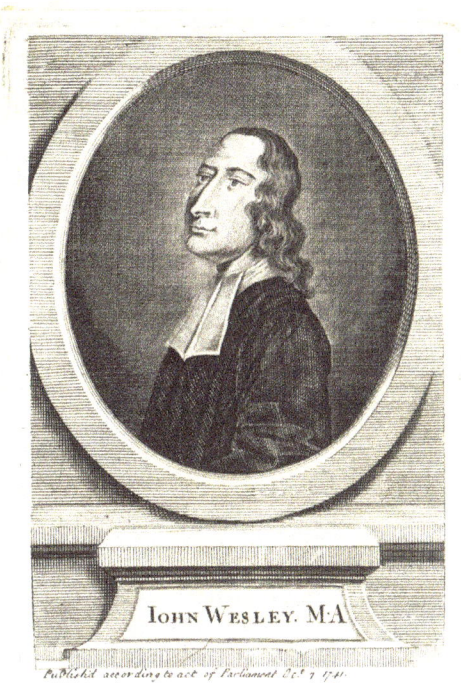

John Wesley, by John Downes (1741)

produced a print. If that connection is the case, then one might presume that this engraving is the Downes portrait of Wesley, published on October 10, 1741. The fact that this date is not exactly thirty years before Wesley's comment is not a major problem.[11]

Some of the characteristics that will become familiar features of the young Mr. Wesley's face in these portraits are noticeable in both of these early engravings: the long nose, the dimpled chin, the thin lips turned up on the ends in a slight smile, and the clerical garb, including Geneva bands.

---

11. Wesley was often only approximate in such instances, such as his saying in October 1771 that he had preached his first sermon at South Leigh forty-six years earlier, when in fact the manuscript evidence of the time pinpoints his having preached that sermon there in 1727, in fact the ninth preaching of that "first sermon" (not the first preaching of that sermon, which was in 1725). Heitzenrater, "John Wesley's Early Sermons," *WHS Proceedings* 37 (Feb. 1970): 112; see also *Journal & Diaries V*, in *Works*, 22:436.

Wesley the Oxford Don

*T*he earliest known painted portrait of John Wesley was also in 1742, by John Michael Williams. At the time, Wesley was still in his late thirties and, as has been pointed out, working in the shadow of people like George Whitefield until well into the 1740s. But Wesley was becoming well enough known that Williams seems to have produced this painting as a private means of procuring income for himself. Advertisements of the day indicate that the portrait was to be exhibited at the artist's home, probably in order to sell the piece.[12]

The Williams portrait is rather fulsome, with a draped red curtain in the background, shelving filled with imposing tomes on Wesley's left, a large edition of the "Holy Bible" on the desk in front of him, and a copy of volume two of the *Book of Homilies*, of the Church of England, held vertically under Wesley's crossed hands in front of him. Some crumpled papers, perhaps notes, appear under the edge of the large tome on the desk. The setting is clearly scholarly with the library of large volumes on the shelves. The context seems religious, given the clerical collar with Geneva tabs that he is wearing, but there is no hint of an ecclesiastical setting, so the occasion is an academic lecture—ordination was a requirement for most teaching (tutorial) positions at Oxford University and the required curriculum was based on a mixture of classical and religious works. Wesley's hair is portrayed as dark, but with hints of the auburn color that was remembered later by Philip Thicknesse, who had been Wesley's housemate in Georgia. He is portrayed as the scholarly Oxford don, having graduated with a baccalaureate and master's degree from Christ Church and being now a Fellow of Lincoln College, where he tutored pupils.

---

12. Advertisement in the *London Evening Post* in September 1743. See Timothy Clayton, *The English Print, 1688-1802* (New Haven: Yale University Press, 1997), 60.

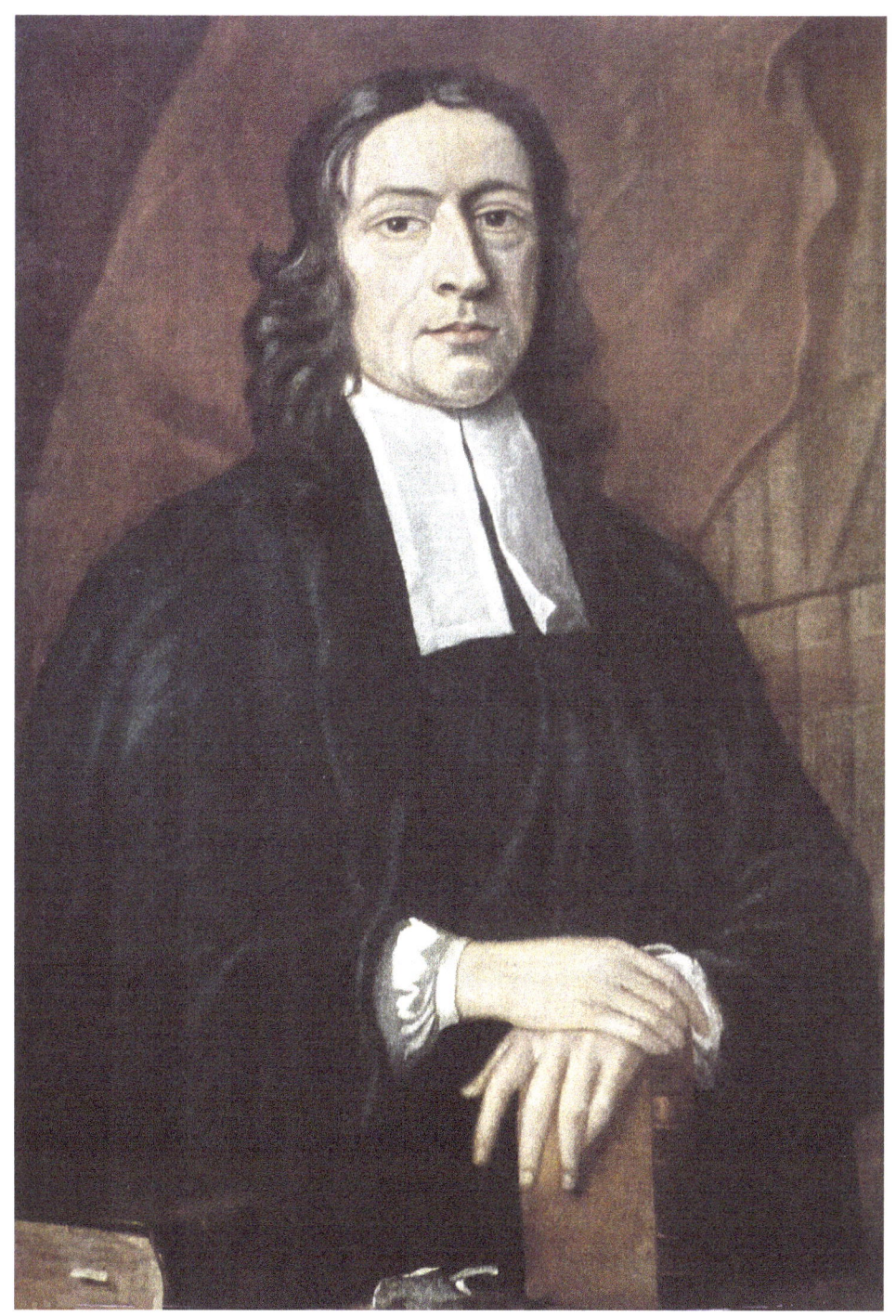

John Wesley, by John Williams (1742)

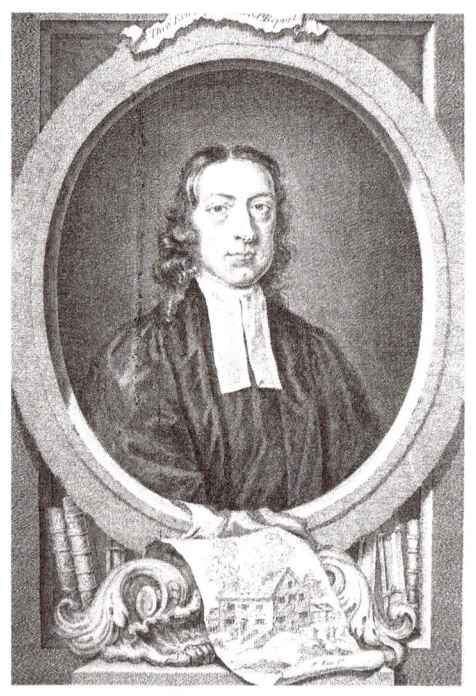
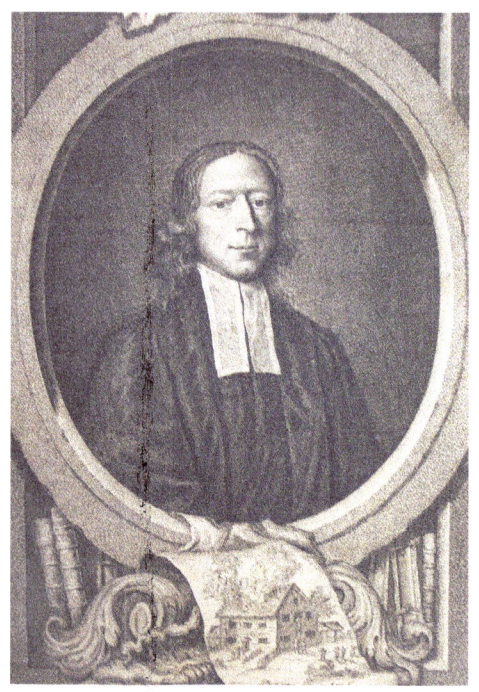

Vertue, State 2   Vertue, State 3

Other artists began to copy this 1742 Williams portrait and
especially began to use Williams's portrayal of Wesley's face
as a model for their own work. Vertue, who had already done
one or two engravings, produced two new versions in 1745:
a published edition and a proof copy. Although these portraits
were contained in the same oval as before in 1742—with books
on either side at the bottom, not in the background—and these
engravings also had the same ribbon motto at the top and the
same vignette of the Epworth rectory fire and caption at the
bottom (similar to his earlier 1742 engraving), the portrayals of
the face were markedly different from his earlier versions (see
p. 6 above) in several ways. The second state of the engraving,
published and dated 1745 in the engraving itself, refines the
printing on the lower vignette, but alters the face itself so that
it matches very closely the Williams painting. Williams is now
noted on the left bottom as "pinxt"—painter. In the second of
these new ones (state 3), the proof copy dated 1745 in pen
and sequenced by close examination of the alterations, the
artist tries to combine his earlier two versions of the face. It is

12

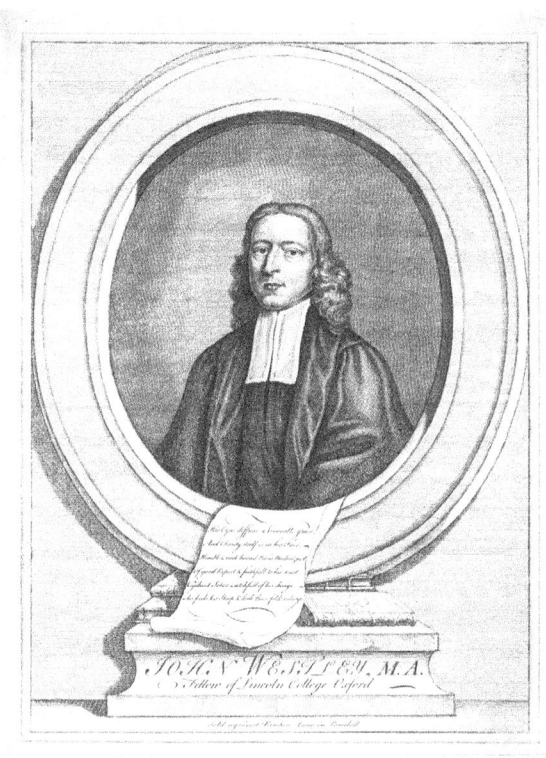

Bakewell ("Moravian" copy), based on Vertue, State 3

softer, more oval than the earlier engraving, and the eyes are dreamier; the hair is not as harshly curly, especially on the top half of the head; the clerical bands are broader and shorter; and the gown has a different configuration—especially the folds of the material in the right shoulder. In most of these changes, the new version seems to have been influenced by his own earlier version as well as the Williams portrait.

This proof, dated 1745, bears a remarkable resemblance to another engraving produced about the same time except that in the new copy the oval outline is simpler, leaving off the ribbon, the saying at the top, the books under the oval, and the vignette of the burning Epworth rectory. The scroll and the subject, however, face in the opposite direction, which is often the result of copying, since the traced drawing, when engraved on a plate, produces a print in the opposite direction. The scroll at the bottom of the oval frame contains an excerpt from a poem purportedly by Emily Wesley instead of the vignette of the Epworth rectory fire.[13] The relationship between the two is still a matter for conjecture, but the caption on the latter, the "Moravian" engraving, states clearly that it was produced and sold by Thomas Bakewell in Cornhill,

13. Located in the collections of the National Portrait Gallery, London; listed as by an anonymous engraver. The poem reads,
His eyes diffuse a venerable grace,
And Charity itself is in his face;
Humble and meek, learned, pious, prudent, just,
Of good report, and faithful to his trust;
Vigilant, sober, watchful of his charge,
Who feeds his sheep, and doth their folds enlarge.

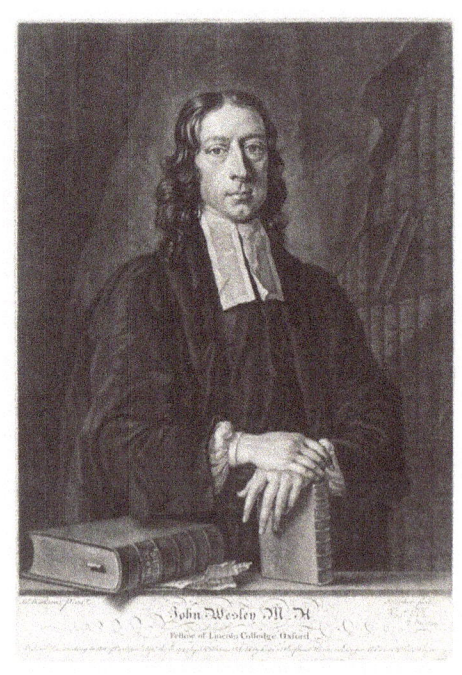

James Faber engraving of Williams's
painting (1743)

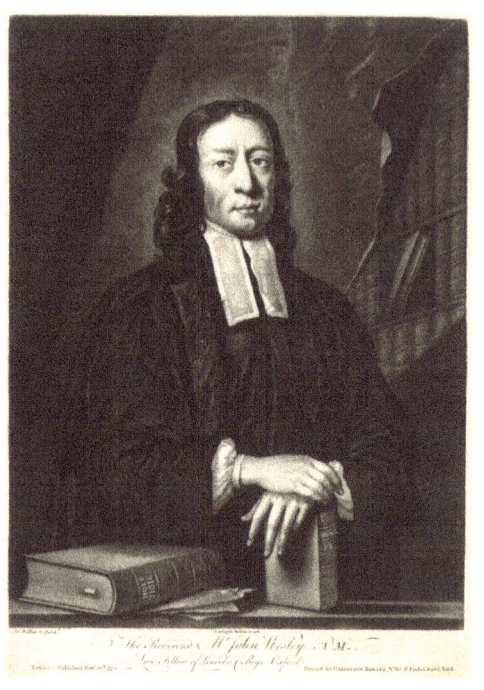

Carington Bowles produced this
mezzotint copy as late as 1770.

James Watson engraving of Williams's
painting

Richard Houston restrike of Watson's
engraving, published by Bowles

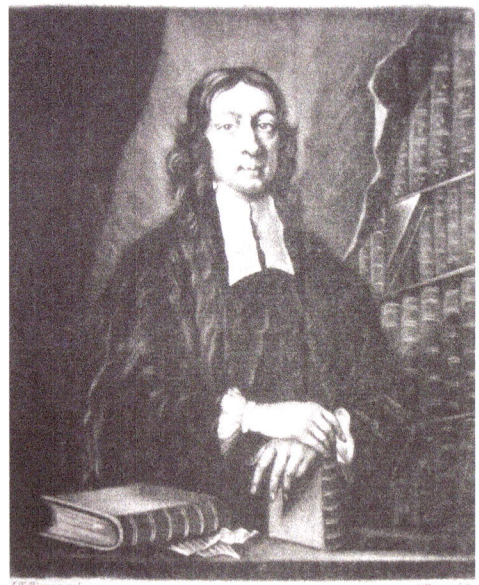

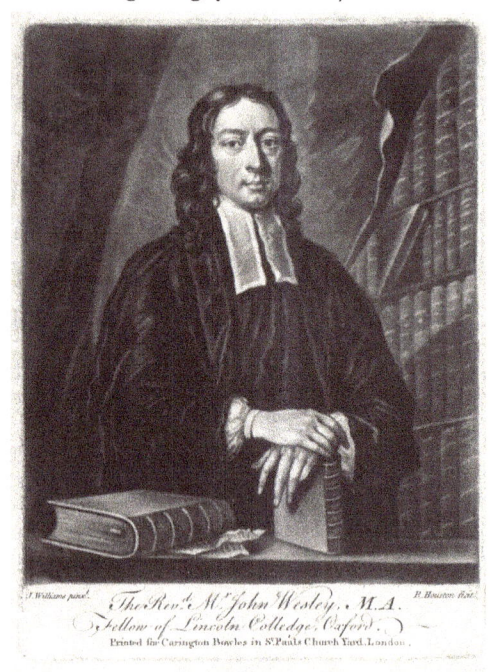

14

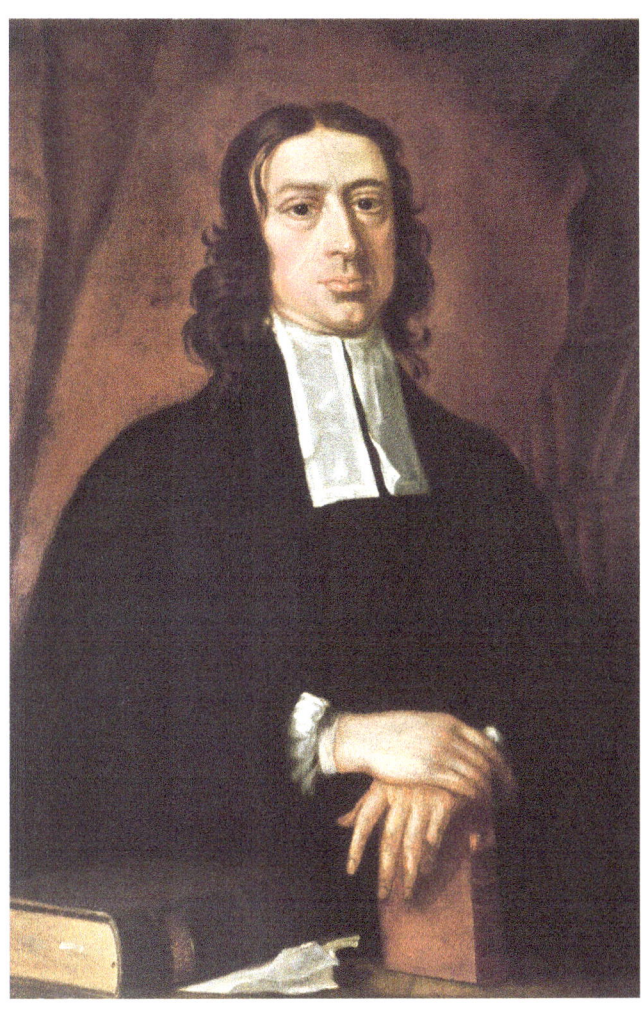

The Harley painting of Wesley (the "Mission House" copy, c. 1745), using the Williams painting as a model.

the location of many printers and sellers of books, maps, and portraits.

Other engravers such as James Faber (1743) produced copies that were quite faithful to the original Williams painting, which became the favorite for engravers to reproduce for more than a decade, with some prints being re-struck as much as thirty years later. Most engravers gave credit to Williams as the painter (pinxt). Copies also by James Watson, Richard Houston, and others altered the face only slightly, sometimes softening its features and making the Oxford don's visage a bit more friendly.

The three-quarters-length Williams painted portrait of Wesley of 1742, library books and red drape in the background, with books on a table in front, was reproduced fully by John Harley, perhaps in 1745.[14] The portrait is known as the "Mission House" portrait, referring to its twentieth-century location in London. It is remarkable for its faithfulness to the Williams model, with only minor differences.

John Harley then painted a copy of his portrayal of Wesley, using only the upper portion of Wesley's image, as it had appeared in the Williams (and later the Vertue) portrait. He

14.   Dated by Kerslake as 1745; Kerslake, 1:302, 2:#856; see frontispiece to this book.

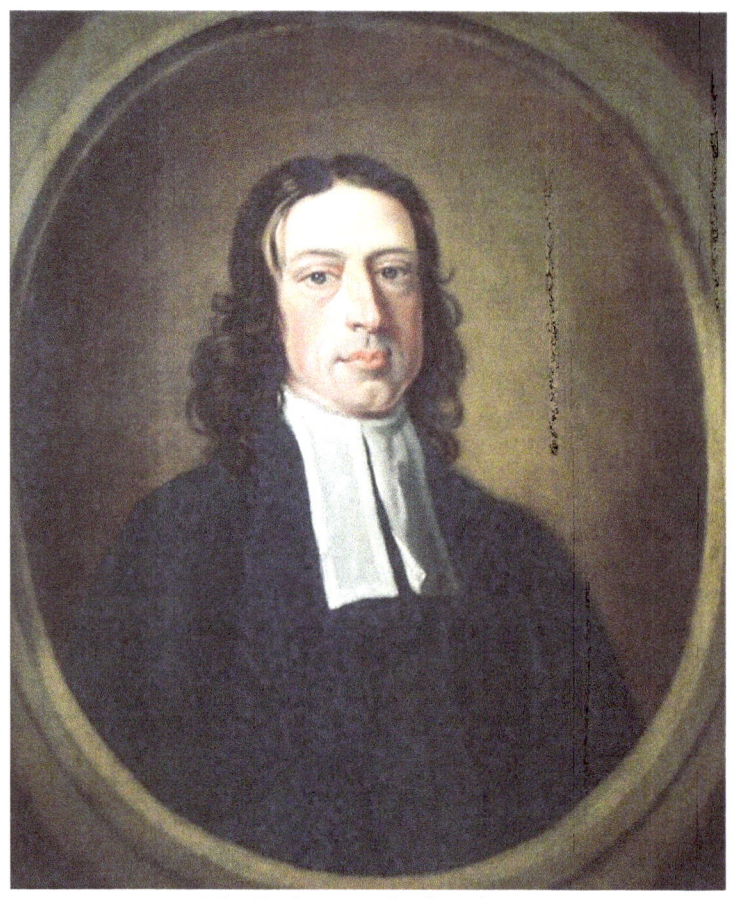

John Harley portrait of Wesley (c. 1745)

removed all the background drapery and library, as well as the foreground paraphernalia, in the Vertue manner, focusing merely on the face. The result was a simple head and shoulders painting similar to a bust. Other engravers and painters then began to produce the Vertue/Harley type of head-and-shoulders portrait with the Williams face.

Mezzotint engravings of this head-and-shoulders version were done by William Faber and later versions by John Tinney and John Haid, although the dates are uncertain.[15] Tinney (1706–61) had apprenticed as an engraver, worked for a time in France, and then went into business on Fleet Street, London, as a print-seller in 1734. He began engraving there before 1741 and apparently sold prints of country houses with Robert Sayer and Carington Bowles in the 1750s. In the decade after his death in 1761, his engraving of Wesley was reprinted from the same plate by Sayer. Tinney had no great ability as an artist, but

15. The original of the first Williams portrait was at Wesley College in Bristol, as was the second, oval version, which is now at the Old Rectory, Epworth. A copy of the rectangular three-quarter-length portrait was produced at an unknown date (perhaps much later) and is presently housed in the "Wesley room" at Lincoln College, Oxford; and the "Mission House" copy is also presently housed at the Oxford Centre for Methodism and Church History at Oxford Brookes University.

made some alterations as he copied the plates, such as altering the length of Wesley's tabs (see also Vertue, p. 12 above).

Johann Jacob Haid (1704–67) produced his closely cropped portrait of Wesley's face in the family printing house in Augsburg, Germany—"A.V." for *August Vindelicorum,* the Latin name for the city.[16] It is one of the few Wesley engravings that bears a Latin caption. On his engraving, Haid spelled the original artist's name incorrectly—"Wiliams."

The Williams rendition of Wesley's face by that time had become the model of choice for the other engravers who were producing pictures of Wesley during that first decade or so, although many of them left out the books, following Harley and Vertue, and used a head-and-shoulders approach.

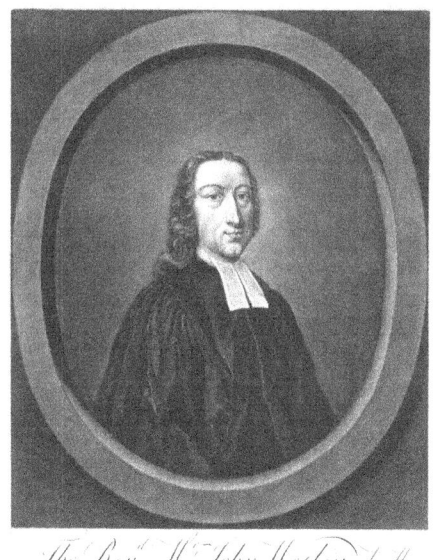

John Tinney's head-and-shoulders engraving has an excess of space within the oval frame.

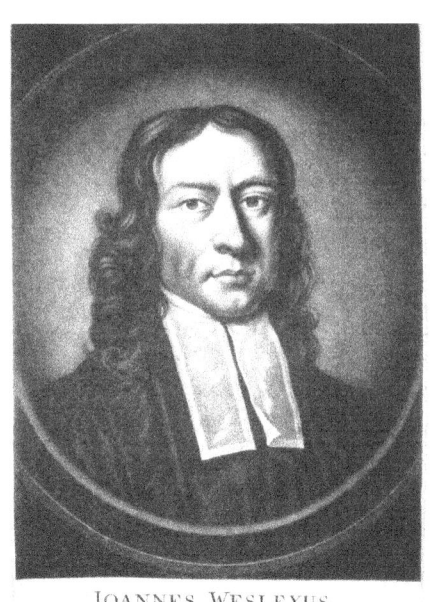

Johann Haid, portrait of Wesley based on the Williams/Harley face of Wesley

---

16. See Frank Keller Walter, *Abbreviations and Technical Terms Used in Book Catalogs* (Boston: Faxon, 1919), 156.

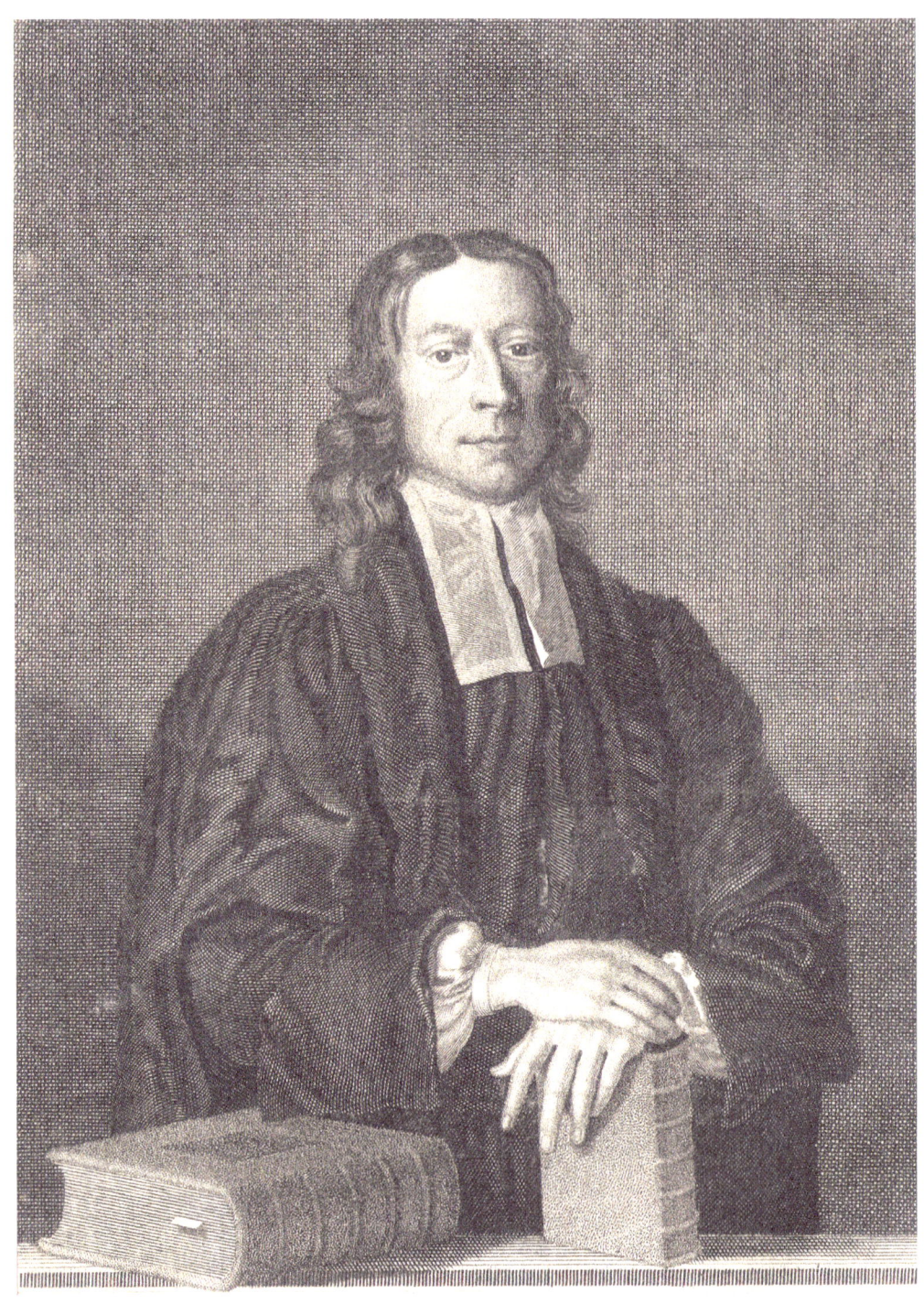

John Wesley, by John Downes (1755)

Methodist personality John Downes also produced an engraving of Wesley in the 1750s. This perhaps second Downes engraving of Wesley's portrait was nearly a replica of the foreground of the Williams portrait, with the features a bit more crudely portrayed. Downes generally followed the pattern of the Williams portrait, including the desk and books at the bottom, but made the setting a bit less scholarly by following the Harley pattern of omitting not only the background library shelves with all the impressive books but also the rather large drapery, leaving Wesley with only a Bible and one untitled publication on the desk in the foreground. This Downes portrayal of Wesley was chosen by the Methodist leader as the frontispiece for the first two editions of his *Explanatory Notes Upon the New Testament* (1755 and 1757). Wesley liked the John Downes copy of the Williams painting. He viewed the engraving as somewhat amazing, given Downes's plain background.

Toward the end of the first fifteen years of these portrayals of John Wesley, then, the Williams portrait had become the defining model for various artists. Often the inscription at the bottom of the picture identified Wesley by name and listed him as a Fellow of Lincoln College, a true fact until 1752. But the age was sometimes listed as older than thirty-nine on some of the later engravings, although the image was obviously a copy of the 1742 Williams painting, which was apparently done from a live sitting at that time.

Although Wesley never mentioned the Williams portrait, the portrayal was just what Wesley would have liked people to consider when they thought of his name: a sober, learned clergyman. That period of the forties and fifties saw many riots aimed at Wesley as a radical field preacher seen by many, especially Anglican clergy, as a ranting enthusiast, rather than the careful scholar of *The Appeals to Men of Reason and Religion* (1745), toward which this portrait leans. Many of the preachers who were being sent back to their trades during this period also saw the Wesleys as hard-nosed autocrats rather than leaders who found their guidelines for spiritual vitality in the Holy Bible and whose services expressed the warmth of God's love, a constant Charles Wesley theme in the hymns. So this type of portrait seems to have filled an important niche in the Wesleyan scheme of apologetic propaganda, not unlike the literary role played by John's published *Journal*.

Wesley as Seen by Critics

*T*he anti-Methodist movement arose about as soon as the Revival began to spread throughout England. One of the most notable of the critics was William Hogarth, who made his living by portraying aspects of British society with which he disagreed, from the gin trade to prostitution to idleness to fanaticism.

In 1761, he engraved a portrait that he called "Enthusiasm Delineated," published the following year as "Credulity, Superstition, and Fanaticism." Among its various notable features that attack Methodism in general, the print shows a preacher in the pulpit with Geneva tabs, thus an ordained priest. Many viewers assumed that he intended it to represent Wesley yelling at the fanatical congregation. Two features that he

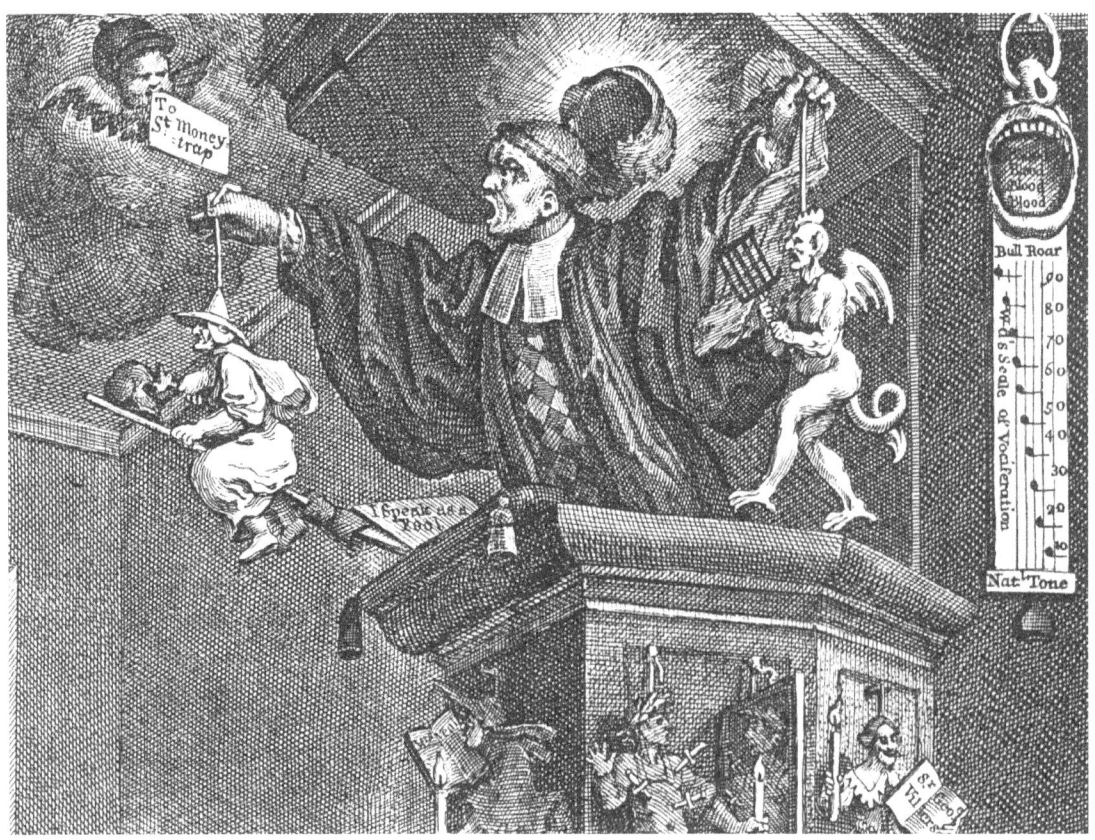

included, however, bring one to the conclusion that it is not John Wesley: (1) the preacher is so animated that his wig is falling off (Wesley did not wear a wig as early as 1762), and (2) the scale on the right, marked from 0 to 100, indicates the "Bull Roar" or "W[hitefield]'s Scale of Vociferation," letting the knowledgeable viewer know the actual identity of the Methodist preacher. The print does take a poke at Wesley also, however, since one of the books shown at the base of the pulpit is the publication of his sermons.

However, another print from a decade later does show Wesley on the title page as

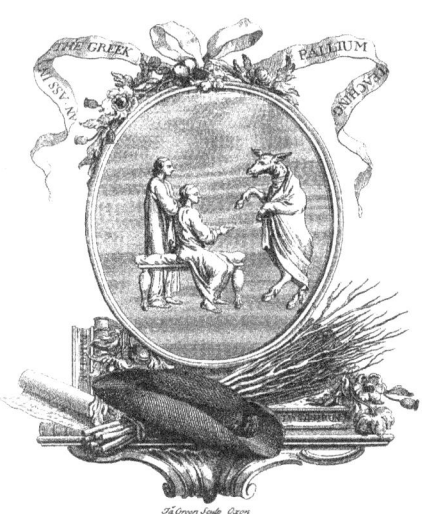

a devil's head, wearing the Geneva tabs.[17] Another small vignette sketch of Wesley's head is on the title page of the satirical poem, "Perfection," also published in 1778. The following year, another long poem in this anti-Methodist series included an engraving by James Green of Oxford, showing Wesley as a poorly drawn fox, teaching his converts.[18] A fourth bawdy portrayal of Wesley in this series depicts him as Reynard the Fox (a preacher with a fox's head), standing on a table in a barn and haranguing a congregation of animals and characters gathered around him. Shown round him are supposedly risqué events from his *Journal*, with citations to the year and page.[19]

These portrayals make little attempt to portray Wesley himself, except to display the Geneva bands and sometimes a robe—very seldom the typical long nose or the curls at the bottom of his hair.

17. William Combe, *The Fanatic Saints; or, Bedlamites Inspired* (London: J. Bew, 1778). The same year, he also published *Perfection, a Poetical Epistle, Calmly Addressed to the Greatest Hypocrite in England,* and *The Love-Feast: A Poem,* among several other satires, using the same publisher.

18. Combe, *Fanatical Conversion; or, Methodism Displayed* (London: Printed for J. Bew, 1779).

19. Ibid., apparently a different frontispiece in some editions; see Heitzenrater, *The Elusive Mr. Wesley,* 2nd ed. (Nashville: Abingdon, 2003), 294 and eleventh plate after p. 208.

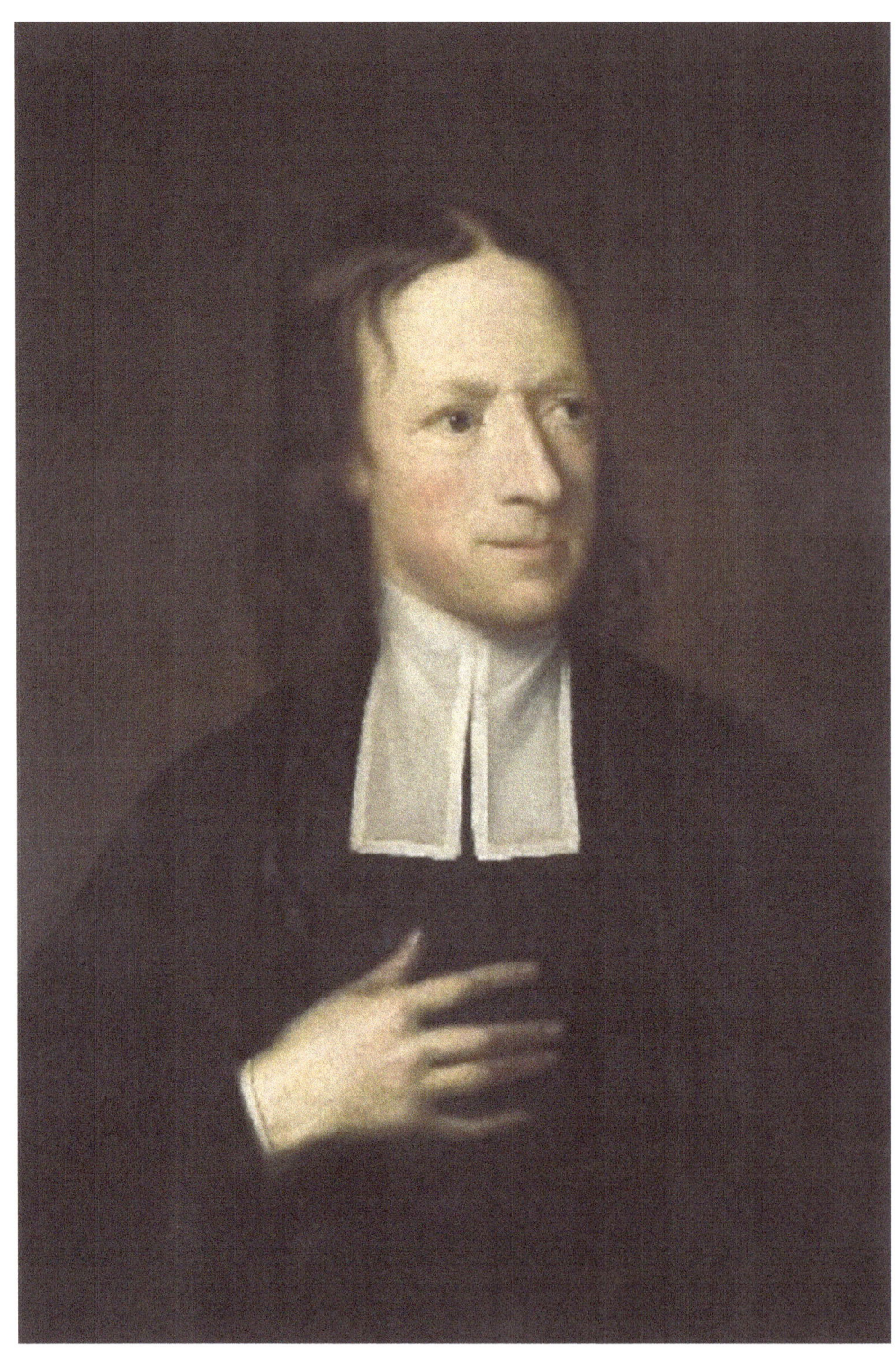

John Wesley, by Robert Hunter (1765)

Wesley the Pious Person

*T*he next major paintings of Wesley were done in the 1760s by Robert Hunter and Nathaniel Hone. Hunter and Hone were Irish artists, the latter eventually settling in London and helping to found the Royal Academy in 1768. Wesley's visage was portrayed during his lifetime by seven academicians of the Royal Academy as well as some Associate Members.[20]

In his journal, Wesley mentions sitting for Hunter "at the earnest desire of a friend" while he was traveling through Dublin at the end of July 1765. It seems that Wesley's sittings for portrait artists, so far as is known, were nearly always at someone else's request. It would be important, in any case, for him to give that impression, even if he did have some desire for such recognition. For one thing (not an inconsequential matter of principle), the other person would then be expected to pay for the process of having the portrait painted.[21] During the three-and-one-half-hour sitting, Hunter finished only the face, a typical beginning point for such a work. Wesley's reaction to the results is notable: "In that time, he began and ended the face, and with a *most striking likeness*."[22]

Perhaps this painting is an example of how little credence should be put in the subject's reaction to the work. Portrait production often entailed flattery, both in the process of the sitting and in the nature of the final painting. Many complaints were lodged that the finished painting was not "a true likeness," and in some cases, the customer simply did not take or pay for the portrait.[23] More than one subsequent commentator has

---

20. The Royal Academy was founded in 1768 with a limit of forty members (R.A.) during Wesley's lifetime. Engravers were not allowed to be elected at first, but were soon allowed to become Associate Members (A.R.A.).

21. Painters charged between 20 (Romney) and 150 (Reynolds) guineas for a portrait during this period. Pointon, 50.

22. *Journal & Diaries V*, in *Works*, 22:15 (emphasis added).

23. Pointon, 48, 50.

reacted to Wesley's evaluative statement by pointing out that the likeness thus portrayed does not bear much resemblance to any other portrait of Wesley. In fact, it portrays him as much younger than Hone's picture, which was painted at almost the same time. Most of the portraits do share some common elements: the presence of Geneva bands, the long nose, and in this case, the stray strand of hair on his right temple, which is present in many early portraits such as the Williams, though here perhaps somewhat exaggerated. The slightly furrowed

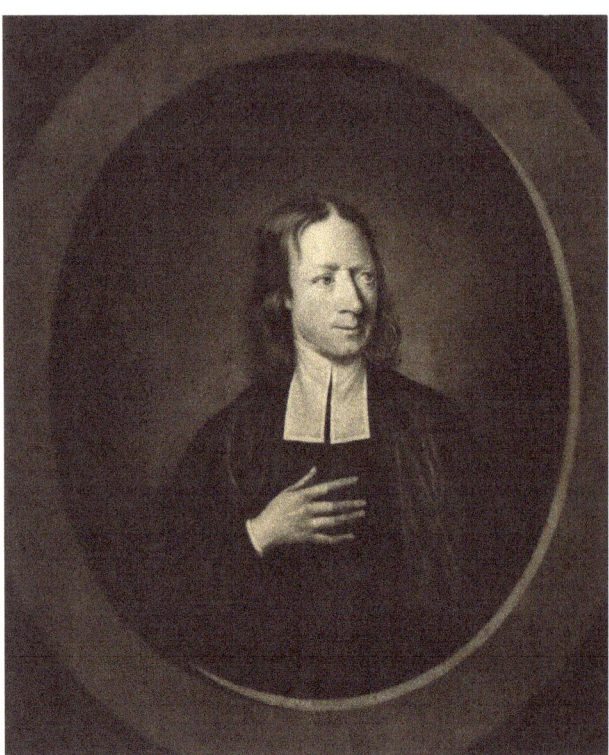

brow, somewhat paunchy cheeks, furtive glance to the side—as though worrying about how long the artist is taking—and strange positioning of the right hand over the heart, perhaps indicating his "warm heart" (with fingers three and four closer together than the other three), are new features in this painting.

Joseph G. Wright, in his article on the Wesley portraits, indicates that Hunter's reputation would not have had much claim to excellence if it rested upon this one portrait. Wright makes the further observation that "Wesley's judgment of it only shows how bad a judge of his own likeness a man sometimes is."[24]

The original canvas apparently disappeared from sight nearly ninety years ago.[25] A copy of the portrait was also engraved in mezzotint by James Watson and published in 1773 (see above).

24.   Wright, *WHS Proceedings* 3 (1902): 185-92.

25.   A later copy hangs in Wesley's Chapel; see p. 25 on left, shown in oval form, the preferred shape for the Hunter portrait reproductions ever since Watson used it.

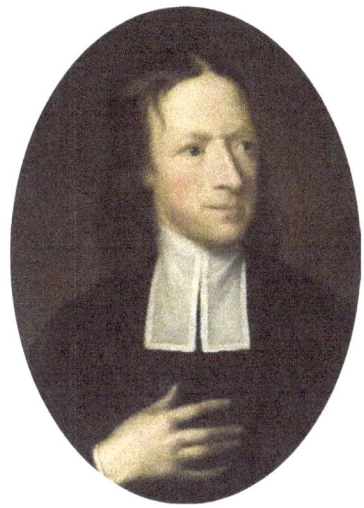

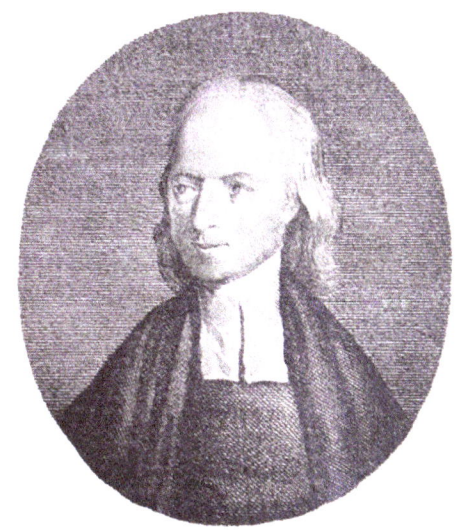

| Wesley's Chapel copy of Hunter | Engraving of "Ranmoor" copy of Hunter |

A rather primitive, if not lugubrious, copy (without the pious hand across the chest) was painted subsequently, known as the "Ranmoor" portrait, since it hung for a time at Ranmoor College, Sheffield. A somewhat crude engraving of it was portrayed on the title page of *The Beauties of Methodism*, published in 1785. The engraving is typical of many copies in that it flips the picture horizontally, the result of using tracing paper to copy the original, and then transferring the image to an engraved plate, which reverses the image thus incised (see p. 92–93).

More recently, the Ranmoor portrait has been owned by Victoria College, Manchester. Its primary feature, perhaps, is the fascinating absence of a typical shoulder line.[26]

---

26. Another later copy, known as the "Poxon portrait" (since it was owned by the Poxon family) includes Wesley's right hand across the chest, but has it very awkwardly positioned with the palm up. The copyist then added Wesley's left hand lying on an open Bible at the bottom.

Wesley the Preacher

*A*bout the same time,[27] Nathaniel Hone presents Wesley in a new way and does so in a rather convincing fashion that provides an alternate model for many subsequent portrayals—namely, rather than the scholar behind a desk and surrounded by books, Wesley is portrayed standing outdoors in a preaching pose, Bible in one hand and the other hand raised in typical homiletical fashion. The artist makes the point that Wesley is actually using the Bible since his forefinger is placed in the book, holding a particular place from the Old Testament for his text. This painting was executed in 1766, which makes one wonder why more than twenty years passed after Wesley's notorious field preaching began in the late 1730s before such a setting was used as the background for a portrait.

However, this painting is evidently not an historical representation of those earlier times, since Wesley's face in the painting is definitely that of a sexagenarian, with the expected facial wrinkles and eyes that look tired and a bit squinty. The setting in the midst of wild trees and bushes was appropriate not only given Wesley's history of field preaching (although that period of his life had generally ended) and the growing interest of the times in representing the drama of nature, but also because he had just published a two-volume natural philosophy entitled *A Survey of the Wisdom of God in Creation* in 1763. The only "unnatural" aspect of the painting is the fact that Wesley's mouth is closed—not something that would generally happen much during his preaching but a common feature of most portraits.

Both Hunter and Hone were respected portrait painters. The former was one of the more prominent portrait artists in Dublin during his time, and Hone, as has been said, became a founding member of the Royal Academy of Arts in London shortly after

---

27. Early engraved reproductions include in the caption the note "Ætatis 63" (age sixty-three; that is, during the year after June 1766).

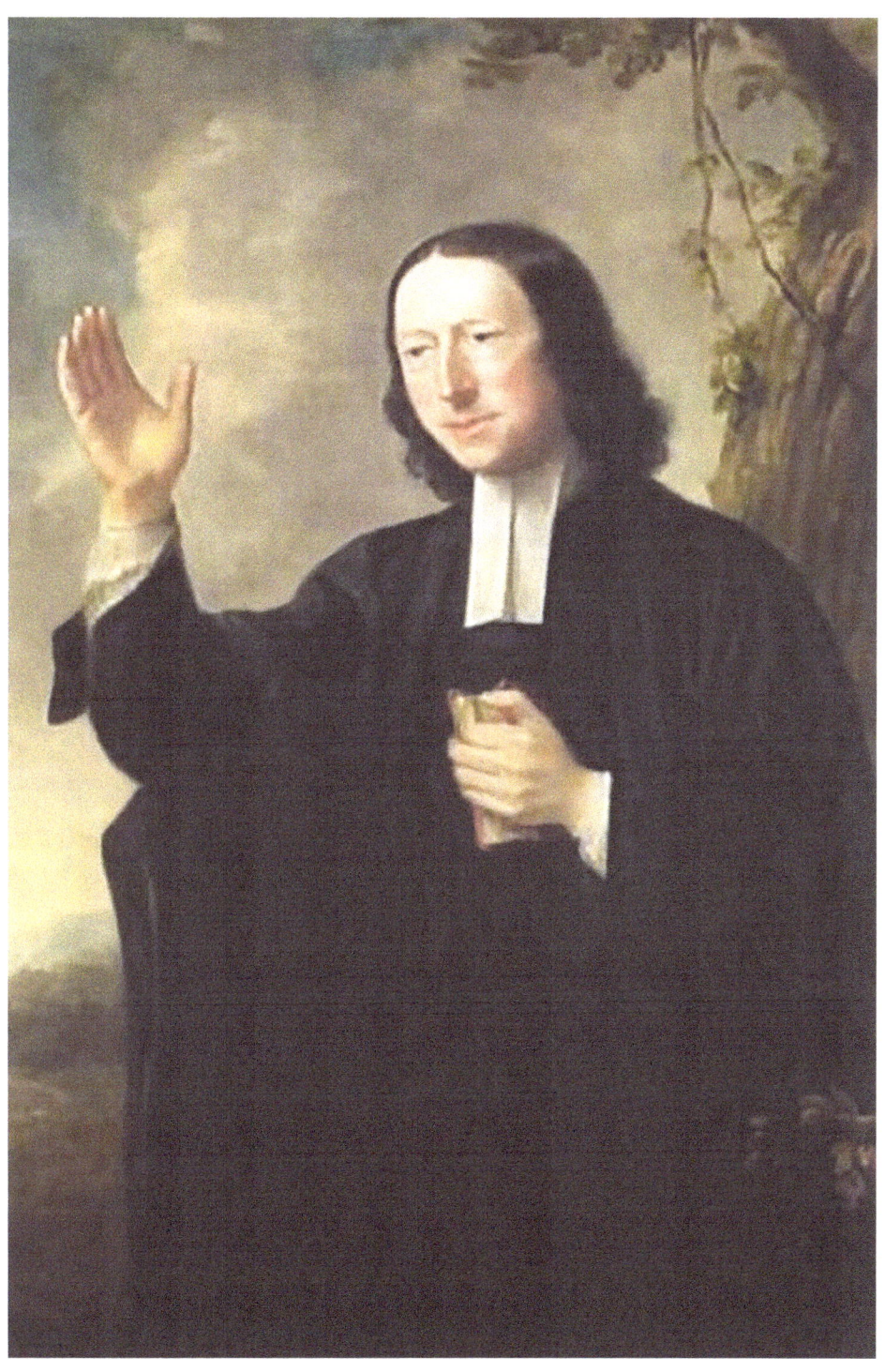

John Wesley, by Nathaniel Hone (1766)

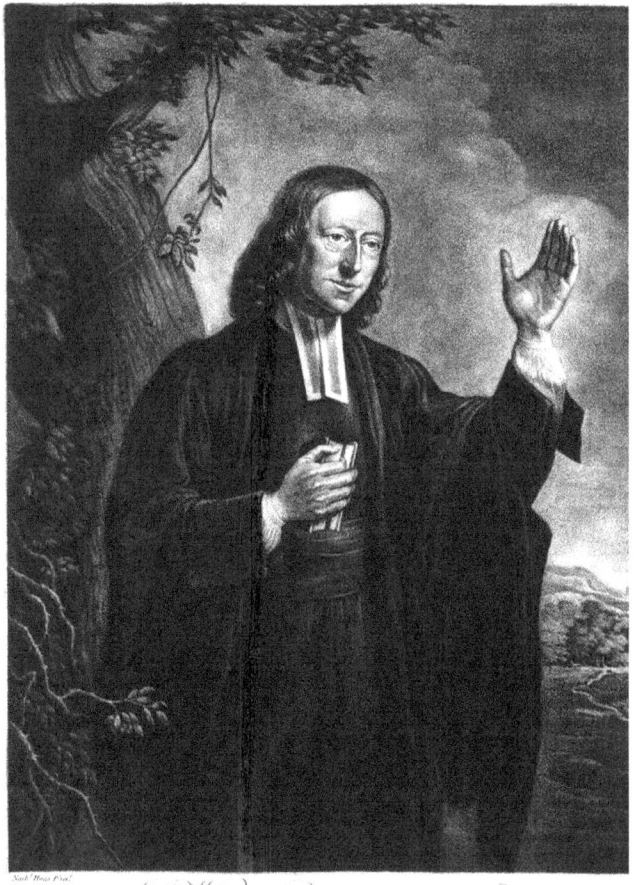

John Wesley, M.A. Fellow of Lincoln College, OXFORD
Chaplain to the Right Honble the Countess Dowager of BUCHAN
Done from an Original Picture in the Possession of The Revd Ladys Son of Scotland

this portrait of Wesley was completed.[28] There is no record of Wesley sitting for Hone, nor is there any comment from Wesley about the painting or the subsequent portraits that copy this image.

The Hone image becomes the pattern for a fascinating sequence of copies, however.[29] First, the painting was engraved by John Bland, who generally produced decent engraved copies of paintings.[30] The process of reducing the intricacies of a painted portrait to the cut lines of an engraving smoothed the facial skin, opened his eyes much wider, and reduced the impression of Wesley's age from something over sixty to something more in the neighborhood of forty.

---

28. Pointon points out that there were 111 portrait artists alone in London in 1780. *Hanging the Head,* 40. Forty artists comprised the Royal Society, with Joshua Reynolds as the president.

29. The Hone painting in the National Portrait Gallery, London, has holes in the corners, evidence of it having been used by the engravers to make copies and therefore supporting the assumption that it is, in fact, the original; see pp. 75 and 92 below.

30. Engravers, though working independently, were often associated closely with particular painters. Romney's records list the names of engravers to whom his paintings were to be sent. Pointon, 41. Occasionally, the engravers produced prints from their own drawings or paintings, at the bottom of which they were noted as "pinxt. et sculpt." The drawer who might transfer another artist's design on paper for an engraving was often noted as "delin."

This younger-looking visage was then copied by American-born John Greenwood in December 1770, reversing the image for his mezzotint, which was frequently the case with copies.

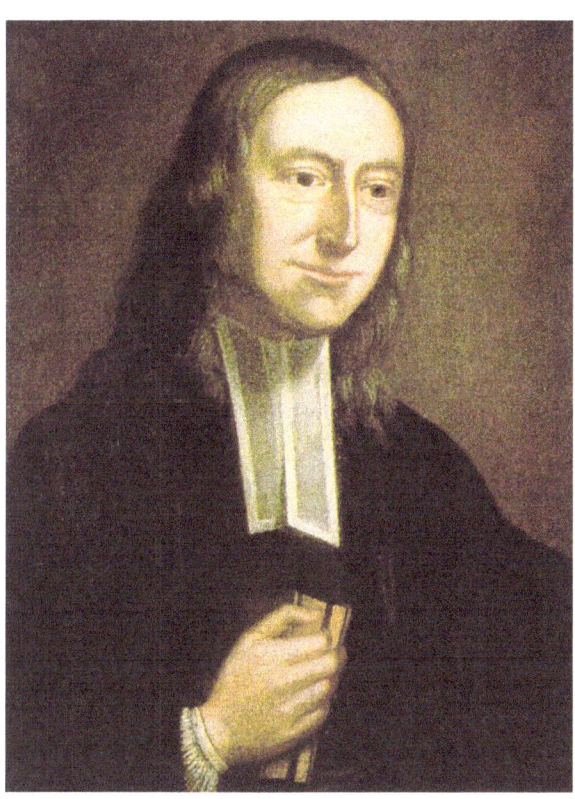
"Cole" portrait based on Greenwood/Hone

The drawing, traced on paper from a print, was then incised on a plate in that position, so that when it was printed, the print came off the plate with a reverse image to the incised image. Greenwood did include all of the romantic accoutrements from nature, as Hone had intended: the clouds, the tree in the background, the rural scene on the side, even the little branch sticking in front of his gown. But the face is smoothed out and made to look much younger, just as in the John Bland engraving of Hone's painting. This is the "sixty-three-year-old" Wesley (somewhat miraculously preserved) that people were beginning to see more frequently portrayed during this time.

At some point after that, the Greenwood-type reversed portrayal of the Hone image seems to have become the basis for a painting by an unknown artist about 1771, according to tradition. This painting of Wesley's face and right hand holding a Bible was owned by John Cole, therefore becoming known as the "Cole portrait of Wesley," and made its way across the sea when Cole emigrated to America in 1785. It thus became known as the first painting of Wesley located in America.[31]

---

31.   This painting is presently housed at Drew University in Madison, NJ. The tradition that Wesley himself gave Cole the painting, along with a letter of commendation to the Methodists in America, is unsubstantiated.

So the whole circle of progress becomes apparent in this one image—from original painting, to engraving, to reversed copy of the engraving, to portrait from the reversed copy. Most of the portraits of Wesley, especially the engraved ones that people actually saw, were copies that were made by artists for whom Wesley did not sit.

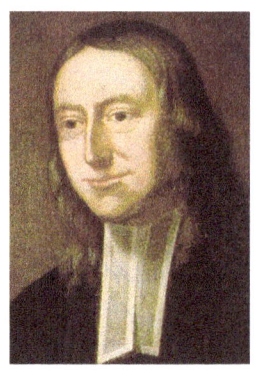

Young face from "Cole" portrait, based on the Greenwood (reversed)

One preliminary conclusion thus becomes apparent: the various portraits of Wesley do not tell us very much about how Wesley looked. They do illustrate a few basic points: he always seems to have worn his clerical garb with Geneva tabs, his nose was quite long and pointed, his hair was kept quite long, and he does begin to garner public notice in the mid-1740s. About that time people are beginning to proclaim him as head of the Methodists, and there are a large number of portraits and reproductions that begin appearing in the following twenty years. There is even a rare engraving by Bland, generally following the Hone painting, that extends the view to full length, showing Wesley sporting tight riding pants![32] The matters of hair color, curls in the locks of hair, type of shirt, pants, shoes, glasses (if any), eye color, position of teeth, and many of the other features of common appearance are not solved by looking at the various portraits.

The question of hair color, along with other matters of color, is complicated by several factors: hair often changes color as one gets older: black or brown often turns lighter to grey or white. Auburn, however, often turns darker, at times looking dark brown or black. Outdoor or indoor lighting, artificial or not, also effects what one perceives in terms of color. The portrayal of reflections can change the artist's or viewer's perception of color, either in life or in the painting. The aging of paints or the fading of inks or the firing of colors on ceramics can often make features such as the color of hair look different

---

32. In this rare engraving, in the Baker Collection of the Rubenstein Library, the lower garment is similar to that shown in the later engraving of John visiting his mother's grave, illustrated in many sources.

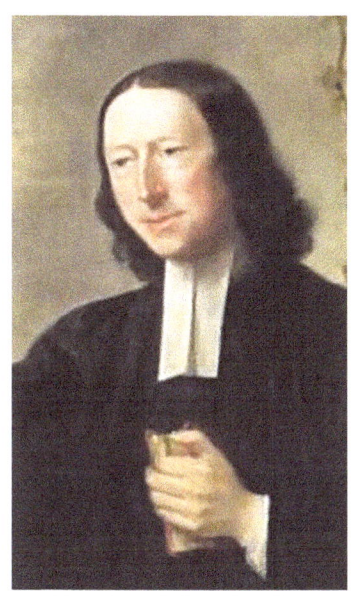

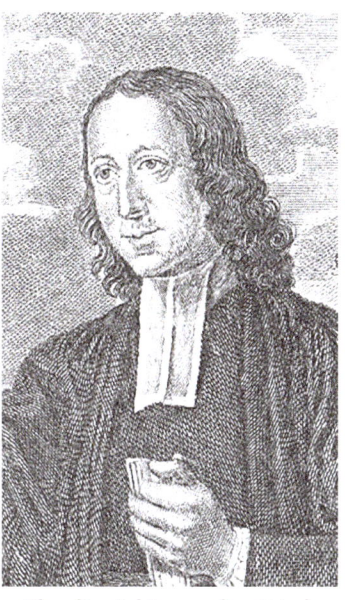

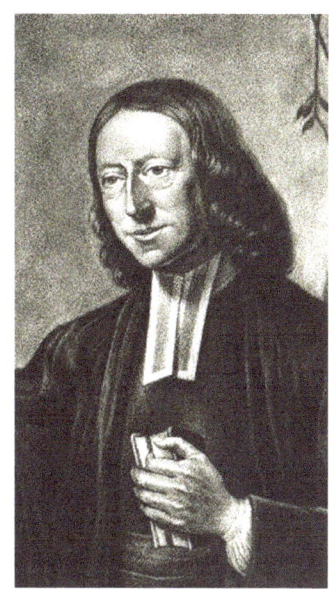

| Hone's painting showing tired lines of a sixty-year-old face | Bland's etching makes Wesley look much younger (frontispiece for *Notes Upon the OT*). | Greenwood's mezzotint (reversed) with even smoother details than Bland |

than originally intended. A good wig looks like real hair, and yes, Wesley wore one in his later years. Examining the artistic representation of such details of a person's visage is often not a very helpful method to determine such details.

Engravings and etchings are even less reliable methods of portraying details of appearance. The use of lines and cross-hatching, while useful to some extent in showing shading, light, and dark areas, do not show much in the way of details and are seldom colored by water colors, which are often second-hand in any case. The smoothing out of surfaces and the idealizing of nature combine to allow the artist to portray the subject in an approximate but very generalized manner, for good or bad. Drawings, generally using pencils, are not much better, given their scarcity and their black and white nature.

Wesley's actual appearance, therefore, is still somewhat elusive, even after examining all the extant portraits—paintings, drawings, engravings, and etchings.

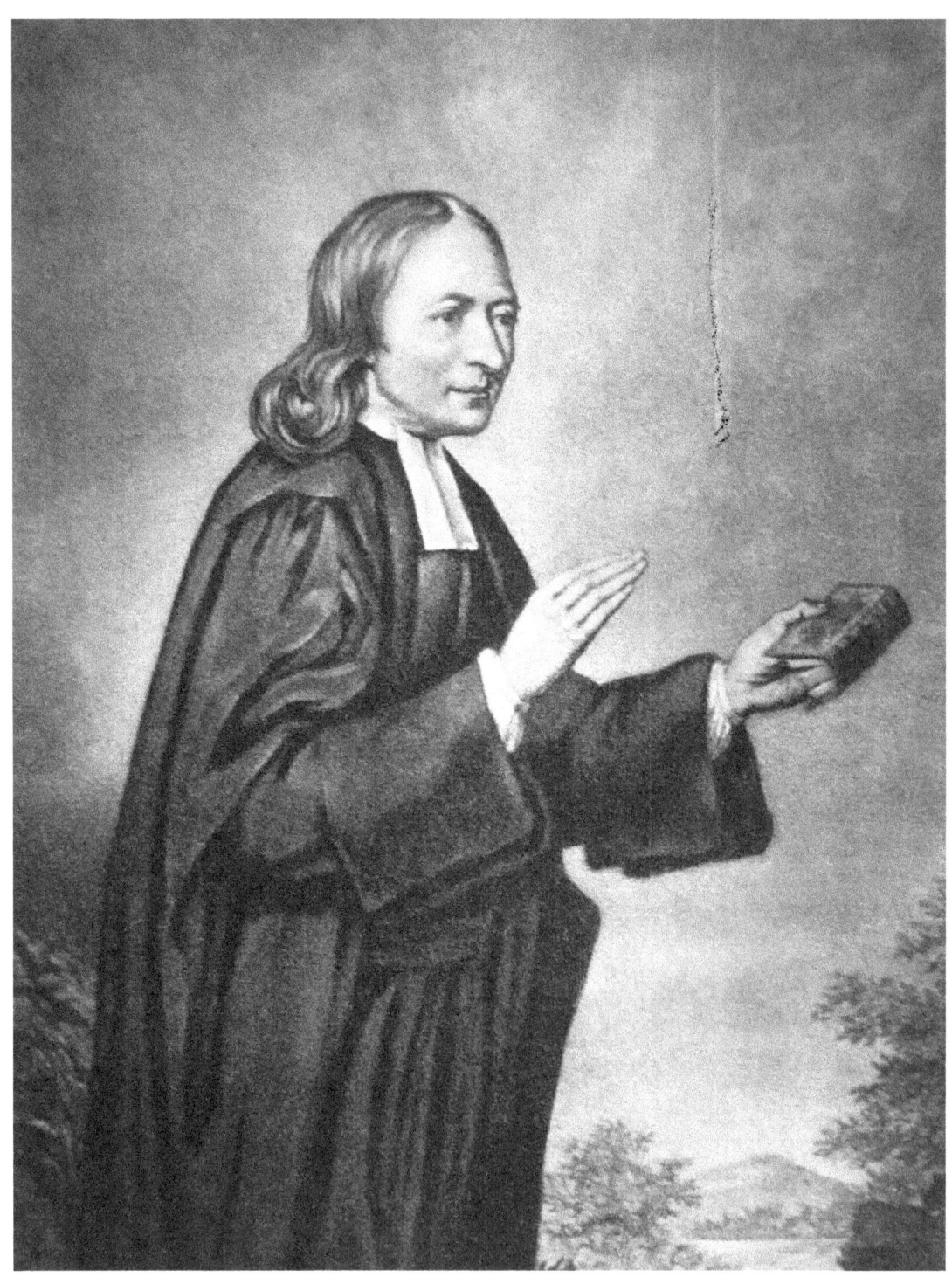

John Wesley, by John Russell, R.A., mezzotint by John Bland (1773)

Wesley the Methodist Preacher

*J*ohn Russell, R.A., was the portrait painter of evangelical leaders—he did paintings of George Whitefield, Lady Huntingdon, Charles Wesley, Charles's sons, and many others. It is not surprising that he produced a portrait of John in the early 1770s.[33] It is also no surprise that he follows the developing tendency, seen in the Hone approach, to show Wesley preaching, and in this case also, preaching outdoors. In many ways, it appears that he knew and used the Hone style as a model: Wesley's left hand holds a Bible, with his fingers holding a reference spot in the texts; the other hand is raised in typical homiletical style; the natural setting is visible in the far background. It may be significant that the two texts being held by Wesley's fingers are obviously from the Old and the New Testaments—both parts of the Bible from which he developed sermons. Though somewhat subdued compared with the Hone portrait, the outdoor setting with trees and other natural accoutrements is not surprising, however, given the other similarities with the Hone model.

The Russell depiction of Wesley's face, however, is somewhat startling, in some ways similar to the way Wesley's face in the Hunter portrait is surprisingly different. In this Russell portrait, the face is much rounder than one might expect, and it is certainly much younger than he would have appeared in 1773, when this painting appeared—he was age seventy. Bland, who had reproduced the Hone image of Wesley, also engraved a faithful mezzotint reproduction of the Russell portrait.

---

33.   It is thought that the December 30, 1771, reference in *Wesley's Journal* is to this painting: "At my brother's request I sat again for my picture." *Works*, 22:303. The painting would have been finished in 1773; the Bland engraving appeared in 1773.

Russell, who painted portraits of many famous people of the time, was a close friend of Charles Wesley's family and painted their portraits. He also produced a painting of George Whitefield, whose tabernacle he attended, during the decade before he painted John Wesley. About the time he painted the latter, Russell was elected an associate member of the Royal Academy and became a full member in the late 1780s, the first Methodist to belong to that august body.

Another portrayal of the Methodist leader is a nearly profile view of just the head and shoulders, a line engraving executed by John Gainer in 1775 followed by a larger mezzotint in 1779. This portrait is not done from life in a "sitting," but is obviously copied from the head of the full-length portrait of Wesley by Russell, minus the raised hand or the other features of the Russell portrait that are farther from the head. So the Bible in the left hand and natural background of trees, hills, and clouds, are omitted by Gainer, who uses the exact same pose, angle, and visage as Russell. He thus changes the mode of the reproduction from a preaching portrait and anticipates that of Wesley the notable person.

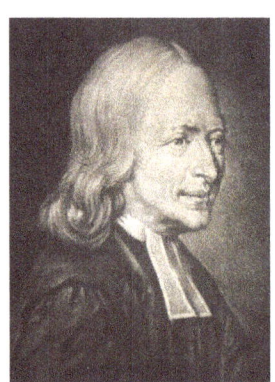

Gainer portrait (1775)

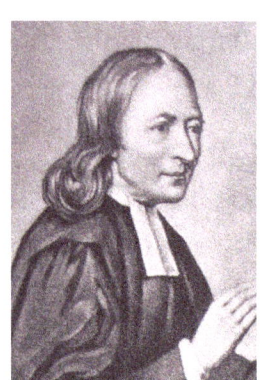

Russell detail

Wesley as Satirized

*T*he early 1775 engraving of "The Pious Preacher," by an anonymous artist and engraver (but perhaps J. Taylor), is a numbered plate produced as part of the "Tête-à-Tête" series of lampoons in the *Town and Country Magazine* published by Archibald Hamilton. The article to which it is attached is entitled "Memoirs of the Pious Preacher and Miss D----mple," tying the anonymous but obvious elderly Wesley, known by the rather extensive biographical details given, to the notorious and eye-turning socialite Grace Dalrymple, said to be twenty-five at the time, in a somewhat scandalous tale. She was painted about this time by Thomas Gainsborough, whose biographer mentioned that "her personal charms were as numerous as her lovers" and that she spent her early life in "exceptionally notorious irregularity."[34]

Since the engraving does show Wesley with his own dark hair, the image is in fact taken before June 1775, when Wesley lost most of his hair as a result of his having a fever. But that also fits the publication date of the "Pious Preacher" engraving,

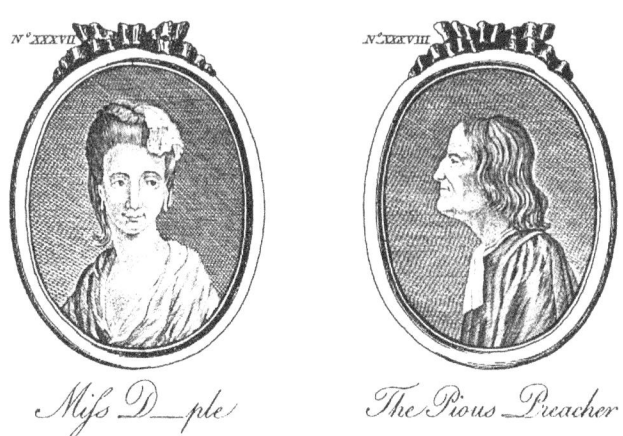

Miss D__ple   The Pious Preacher

Publish'd as the Act directs by A.Hamilton Jun.ʳ near S.ᵗ John's Gate Jan.ᵈ 20. 1775.

---

34. A. B. Chamberlain, *Thomas Gainsborough* (London: Duckworth, 1903), 185-86.

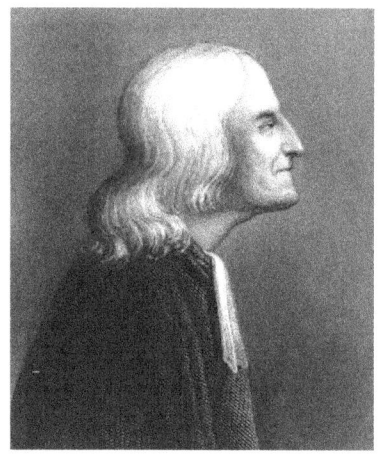

which appeared first in January of that year and then a second time (paired again with the portrait of Miss Dalrymple) in a reprint of the article in the February 1775 issue of the *Hibernian Magazine.*

The same image appears again much later in a portrait engraved by William Greatbach, the nineteenth-century engraver whose work started appearing in *The Art Journal* in 1849, reproducing works by other artists. His image of Wesley, which appears to be taken from "The Pious Preacher" of the previous century, becomes the frontispiece for a biography of Wesley by Isaac Taylor in 1851,[35] although John Telford claims that the original from which it was taken was purported to be

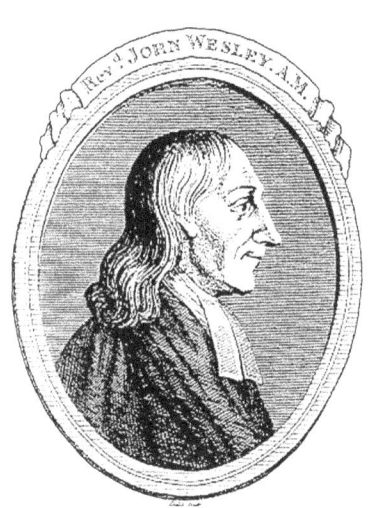

by Thomas Worlidge, R.A., in the mid-eighteenth century, who supposedly took the image from life while Wesley was preaching at the Foundery in London.[36] The Methodists did use the Foundery for services until the Chapel was completed in 1778, three years after the "Pious Preacher" appeared. But the attribution of this work to Worlidge is somewhat conjectural, however, since the artist died in 1766, a decade before that type of image first appeared in *Town and Country Magazine.*

On March 4, 1781, the *Sunday Magazine* included an article on John Wesley in their "Ecclesiastical Mirror" series, which described the character and principles of the popular preachers within each denomination in London. The portrait that accompanied the article was engraved by John Lodge

---

35.   *Wesley and Methodism* (London: Longmans, 1851).

36.   Isaac Taylor was told that the portrait "was taken from the side gallery at the Foundery when Wesley was preaching." John Telford, *Sayings and Portraits of John Wesley* (London: Epworth Press, 1924), 210.

of Holborn (active c. 1754–94) and printed by John Wade of Fleet Street. It is one of the earliest profile views of Wesley, a form that seemed to predominate after his death a decade later. The depiction does not show him preaching, but is a simple head and shoulders portrait, which identifies the subject by putting his name in a ribbon along the top of the oblong frame. The engraving features his long pointed nose, along with the typical long hair (probably natural, not showing the curls of the later wigs) and the Geneva tabs. The portrait bears a direct resemblance to "The Pious Preacher" of 1775 (though reversed direction) and, in a similar fashion, comes close to being a caricature of the man. But the article is a somewhat serious description of his impact on British society, in spite of his being a somewhat despised Methodist, noting in the title that he was, among other things, chaplain to the Countess Dowager of Buchan, a title that Wesley seems to have held (with Lady Huntingdon's help) at least from 1768 through the death of George Whitefield in 1770.

Other attempts to portray Wesley in a satirical fashion are often not in portrait form. The frontispiece to the lengthy satirical play *Fanatical Conversion* is typical in portraying Wesley full-length as a fox, tricking and preying on his people.

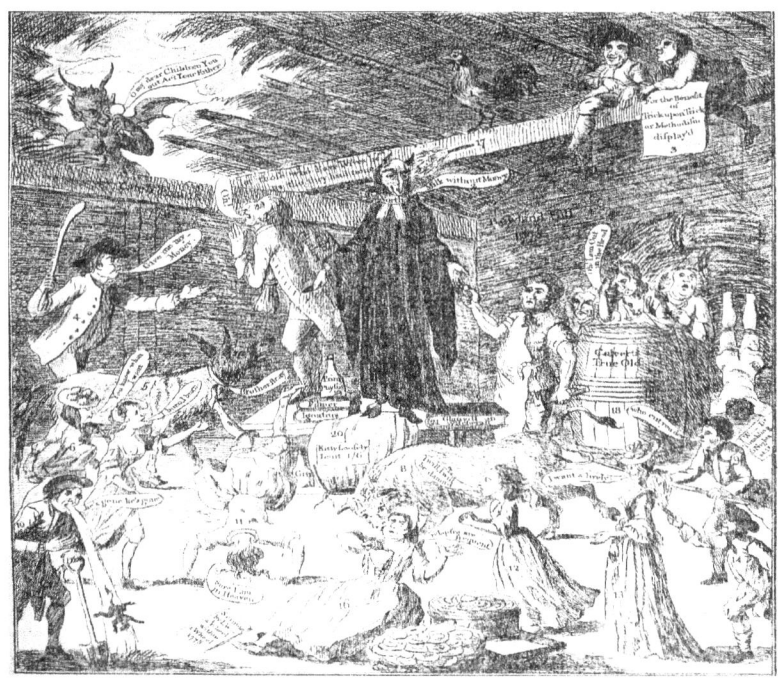

Wesley the Methodist Leader

*W*esley had included very few portraits of himself in his own publications: the Downes portrait, based on Williams, in his New Testament *Notes* in the mid-1750s, and a Bland engraving of the Hone portrait in the Old Testament *Notes* of the mid-1760s. His other attempt to provide such portraits for his reading public came over a decade later.

Although they are not based on any known paintings, the portraits in the *Arminian Magazine* should be mentioned as part of the developments in the 1770s (this part of the story extending into the 1780s). Wesley started the magazine as his answer to the Calvinists, not only to their theology as such—beginning with his struggles with Whitefield in the thirties and culminating with the crisis of the 1770 *Minutes*—but also to their magazines, such as the *Gospel Magazine*. As a frontispiece for the first year's volume of these monthly magazines in 1778, when bound together, Wesley chose an engraving by Bodlidge (a)—one of the strangest portraits of Wesley ever produced, and that under his own watchful editorial eye! One thinks that he might have anticipated the public outcry that ensued, resulting in an apologetic note in the magazine itself and the production of a substitute portrait (b) for those who wanted to replace the earlier one.

This second portrait makes Wesley look much younger than his seventy-seven years of age at the time—perhaps more like thirty-five or forty. He also looks somewhat aristocratic and learned, if not actually suave. Apparently there was no negative reaction to this portrait. Which makes one then wonder why Wesley provided yet another portrait of himself (c) for the readers of the *Magazine* in 1783, which is perhaps even worse than the 1778 engraving. One would be hard-pressed to say why anyone would think this a worthy portrait of anyone, much less one that should be circulated by the thousands, as was the case with the *Magazine*.

In any case, that appears to mark the end of Wesley making such decisions about using his portrait in any of his publications.

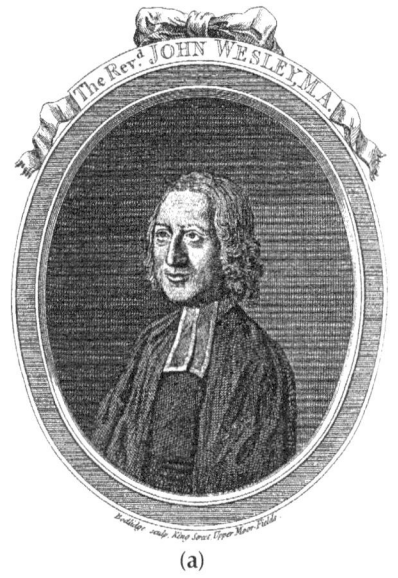

(a)

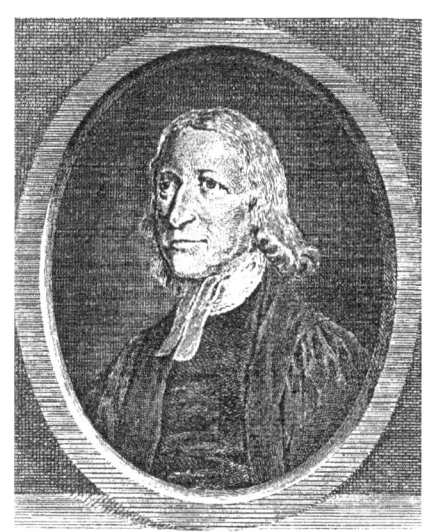

(b)

(c)

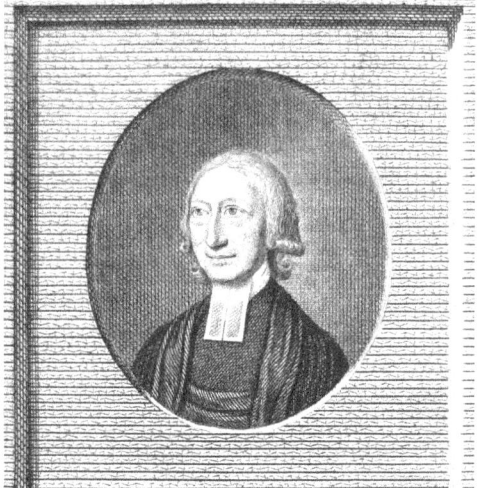

Arminian Magazine portraits of Wesley (1778–83)

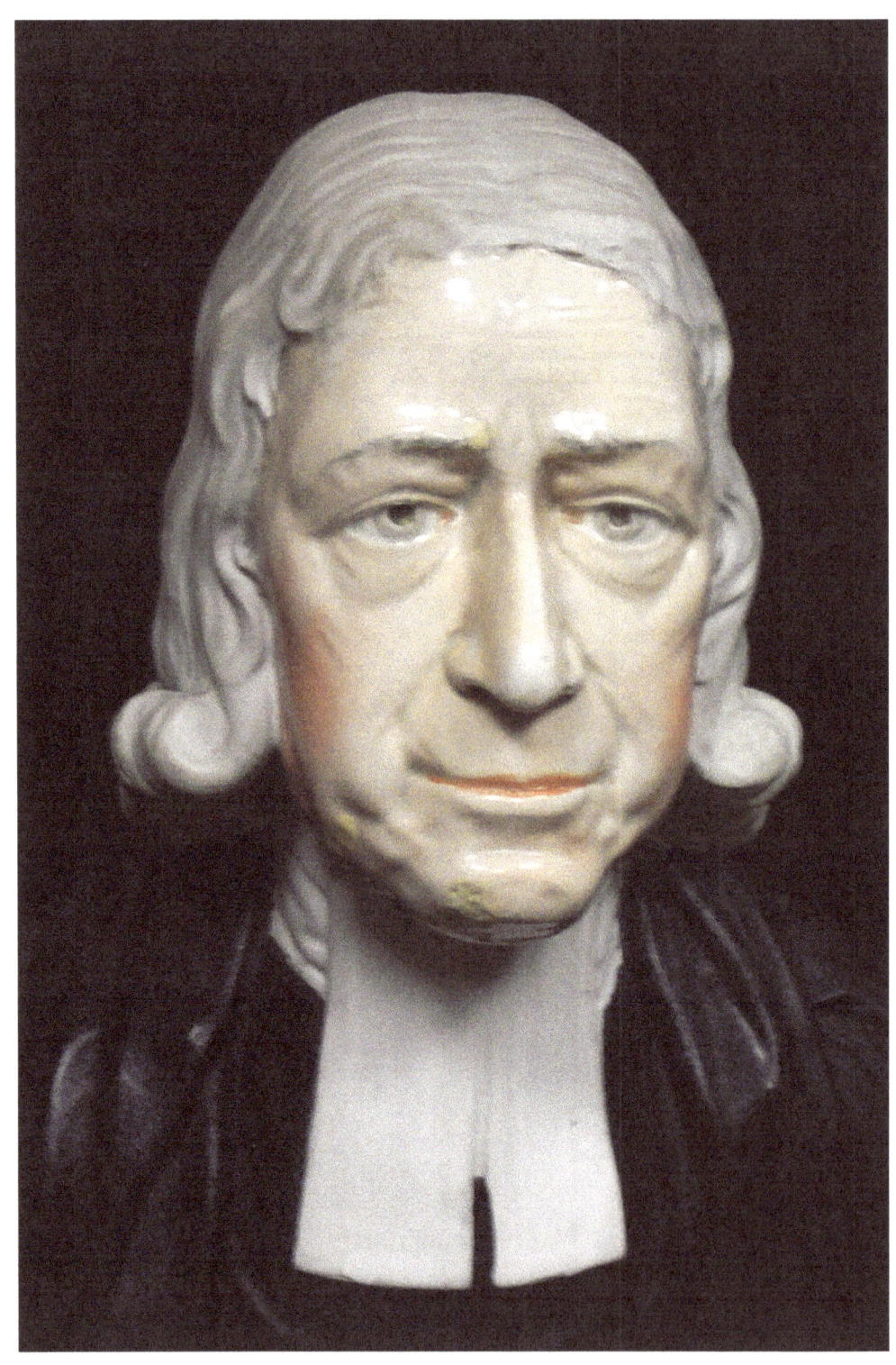

Enoch Wood bust of Wesley (c. 1782)

Wesley as Ceramic Model

In spite of the proliferation of portraits by entrepreneuring engravers and printers for years before and after Wesley's death (both favorable toward and critical of Wesley), many people, including Adam Clarke, felt that Enoch Wood's bust of Wesley, produced in the early 1780s, was the best likeness ever produced of the man, "the only one that could fairly pretend to be compared with the original"—his actual visage.[37] From Wesley's point of view, the sitting lasted an inordinate amount of time, but he was happy with the result.

The subsequent re-castings and firings of the busts over the years (Wood produced several editions himself) has resulted in Wesley's face becoming narrower in the later versions and the head becoming more and more tilted upward. The result is a much more spiritual or pious demeanor, but one not true to the original portrayal. Even with the copies and various renditions over the years, they were never put out in the numbers that engravings were and therefore never were on display in the homes of thousands of faithful Methodist followers, who had one of the various printed iconic images of Wesley burned into their minds if not their spiritual consciousness. The Wood bust of Wesley has been used for generations as a model for paintings of Wesley's face by John Renton, George Zobel, and most successfully by Frank Salisbury in the twentieth century.

Several other ceramic portrayals of Wesley become significant during his lifetime. He became a friend of Josiah Wedgewood, the Staffordshire potter, and the relationship resulted in several renditions of Wesley in ceramic form. Wedgewood was famous for having discovered a method by which thin white ceramic images could be adhered to a green, blue, or black background

---

37. See Nehemiah Curnock, ed., *The Journal of the Rev. John Wesley, A.M.* (London: Epworth Press, 1913, 1938), 6:309, quoted in Kerslake, 1:302-3.

on plates, bowls, pitchers, cups, or nearly any form his shop could produce. The profile image of Wesley that was frequently used during the period of his life was executed by John Flaxman, R.A., and placed on works ranging from cameos to teapots.

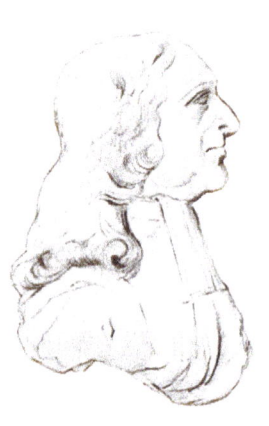 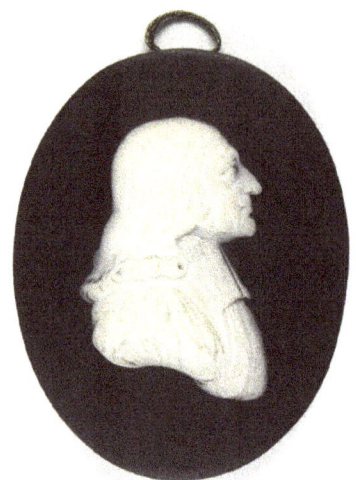 

The Flaxman drawing on the left is shown reproduced on two Wedgewood cameos.

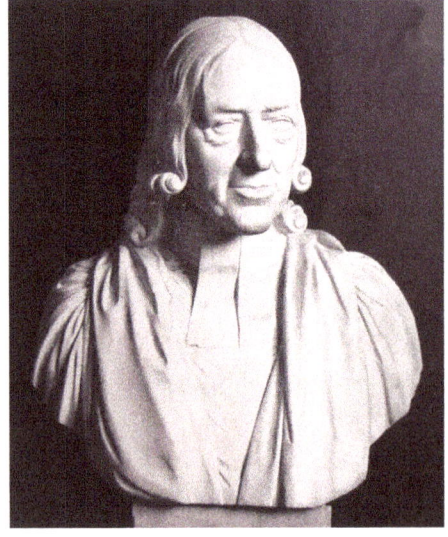

The image that Flaxman used is similar to some of the other profile engravings of Wesley that were produced close to that time in the late 1780s, showing his wig with two rows of long curls. The Wedgewood bas-reliefs provide a sense of mature dignity, if not weariness, that is evident in the Wood bust and many later portrayals, even though they show a fuller face, as is found on the bust known as the "Roubiliac" bust in the National Portrait Gallery, London (left).

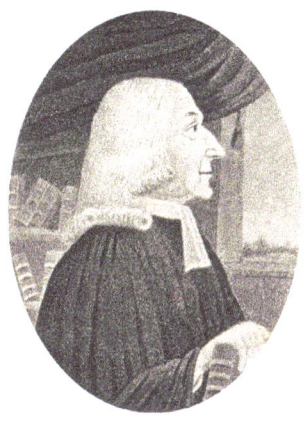

J. Palin (later copy
of Edridge)

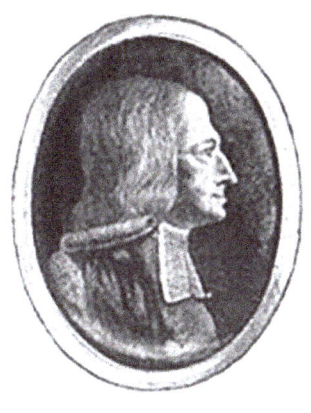

Henry Bone, R.A.,
miniature (1780)

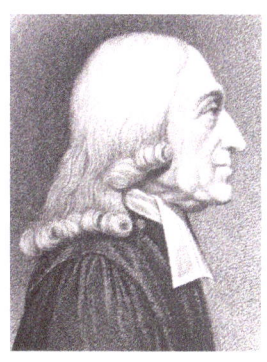

Later copy of Edridge

One element that is also inconsistent in the portrayals of the mature Wesley is the curls on the bottom of his hair or perhaps his wigs. In most cases, there are two rows of curls—one under the ears and the other from there, shoulder length, around the back. But in some instances, the hair is shown as having one row of curls at the bottom, nearly shoulder length from one side to the other. In the Enoch Wood bust, there is very little difference in length, from the front side to the back. In others, the front row is much shorter than the back, but always covering the ears.

The shape of the skull also varies among the profile portraits. The forehead, while usually showing a somewhat receding hairline, often has the lower portion protruding and the upper portion rather bulbous, as in the frontispiece to a book printed in Dublin in 1782 on *Eminent Methodist Preachers,* which reverses the recently done Bone profile. Some, however, have a somewhat severely sloped forehead, such as the Flaxman drawing for Wedgewood. These features are not so evident in the earlier portraits, which tend to be more straight on.

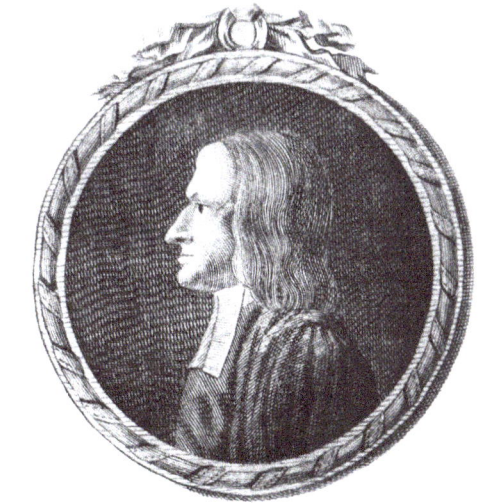

Wesley the Anglican Preacher

*O*ne of Wesley's personal favorites among the painted portraits was the one by William Hamilton, R.A., that is presently owned by the National Portrait Gallery, London. He sat for Hamilton on December 22, 1787, and remarked in his *Journal,* "I yielded to the importunity of a painter. . . . I think it was *the best that ever was taken*." Then he adds the caveat, "But what is the picture of a man above fourscore?"[38]

The portrait shows him preaching from a very nice pulpit with the Bible in front of him, lying on a red velvet cushion. Although there are not the typical accoutrements of a Church of England in the background—reredos, cross, candles, and the like—the plainness of the walls is offset by the presence of the velvet cushion on the pulpit, something that one might not expect to find in a Methodist preaching house. But as has been said, these paintings were not expected necessarily to represent reality, and Wesley himself may have requested the nature of the setting portrayed in the painting, which could be filled in later, after the painter had finished the face.

The right hand raised, palm inward, and the left hand either on or grasping a Bible, is typical of the "preacher" portraits of Wesley.[39] However, Wesley's mouth is slightly open, as though preaching, somewhat calmly—the only portrait of Wesley that shows his mouth actually open. Although it appears that Wesley might be referring to two different biblical passages—his hand seems to be holding another place open—both passages are obviously Old Testament texts before the Psalms, which is not unlikely for a Wesley sermon.

---

38. *Works,* 24:68 (emphasis added).

39. See portraits by Russell and Hone above.

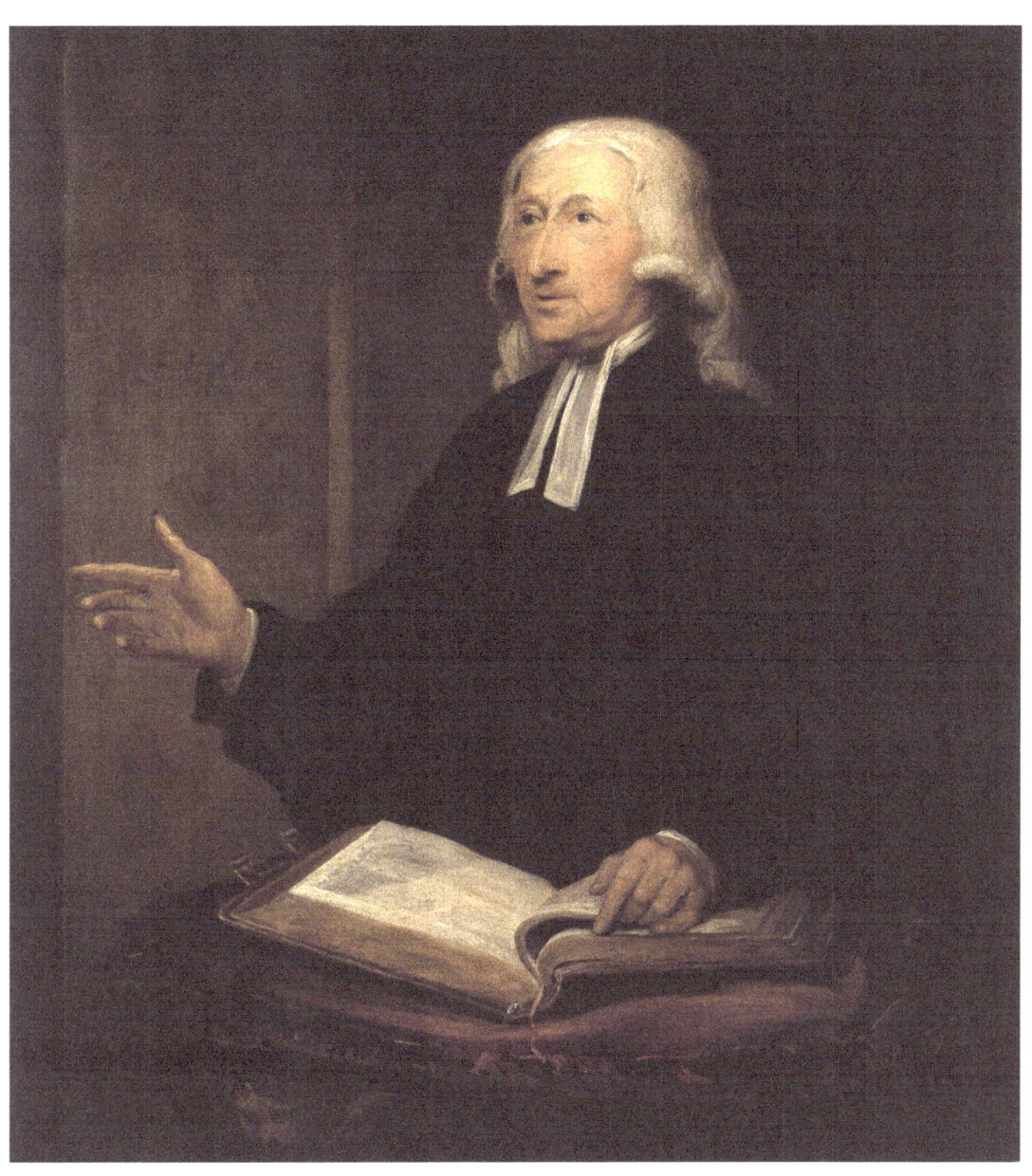

John Wesley, by William Hamilton, R.A. (1787)

Hamilton's painting was reproduced carefully and in grand manner by James Fittler in the same year (1788), with the Wesley coat of arms centered in the caption. This portrait was followed by a later but almost identical engraving by Richard Roffe.

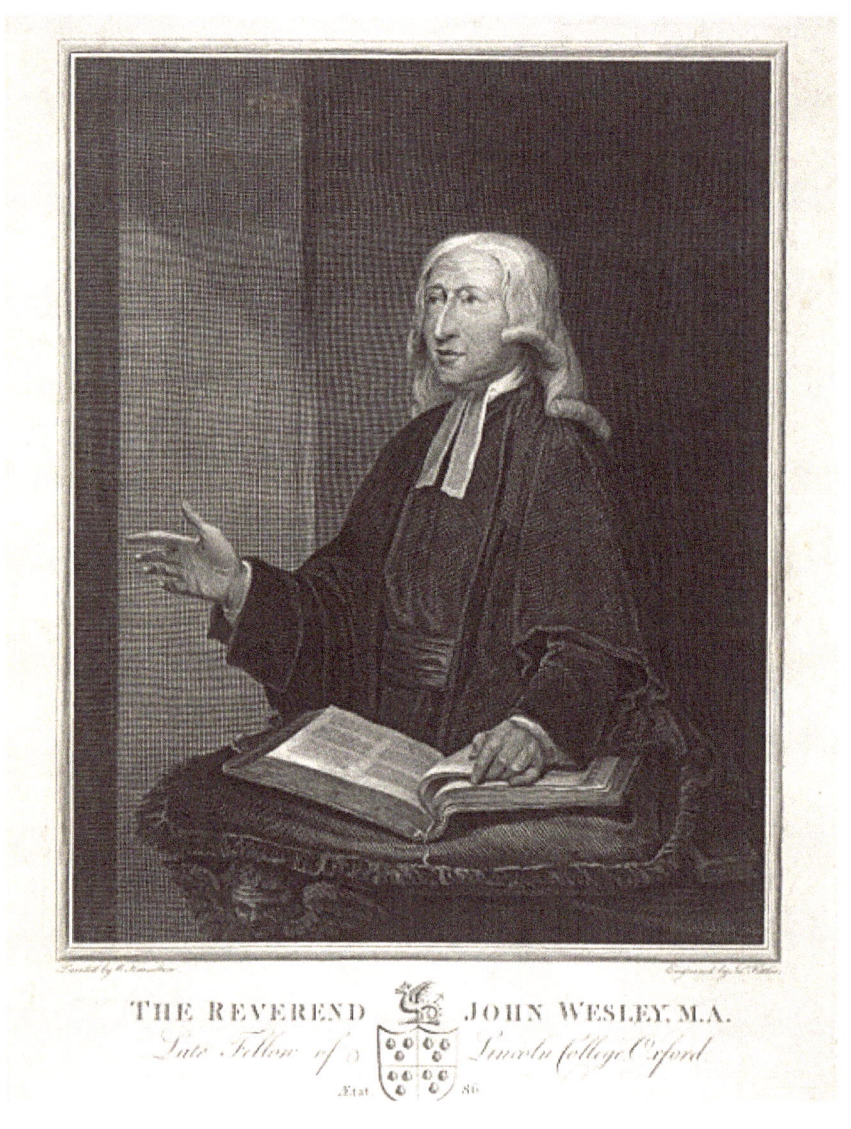

THE REVEREND JOHN WESLEY, M.A.
Late Fellow of Lincoln College Oxford

Engraving by James Fittler (1788)

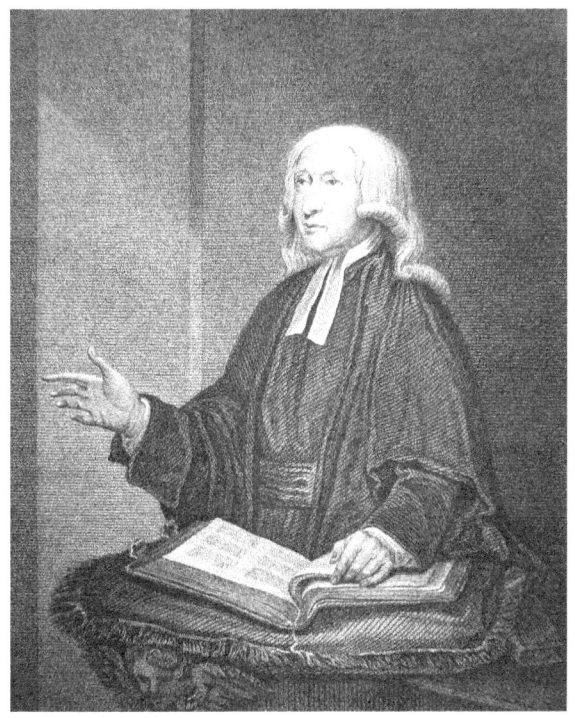

Later engraving by Roffe based on the earlier Fittler engraving

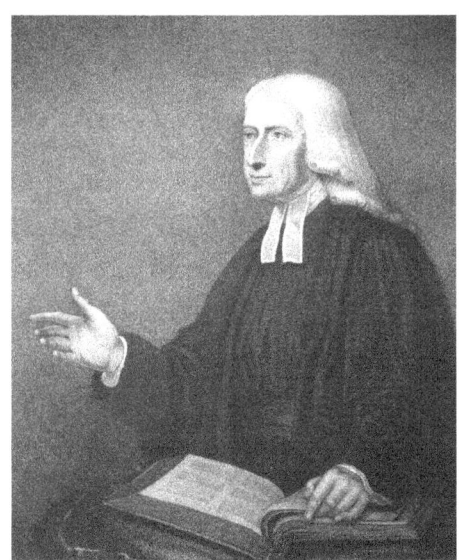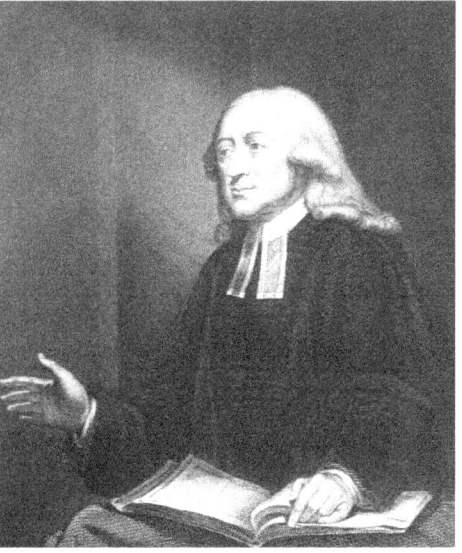

Two unknown artists put two later renditions of the face upon the Hamilton portrait,
one face from the painting by Barry (1791), the other by John Jackson (1827).

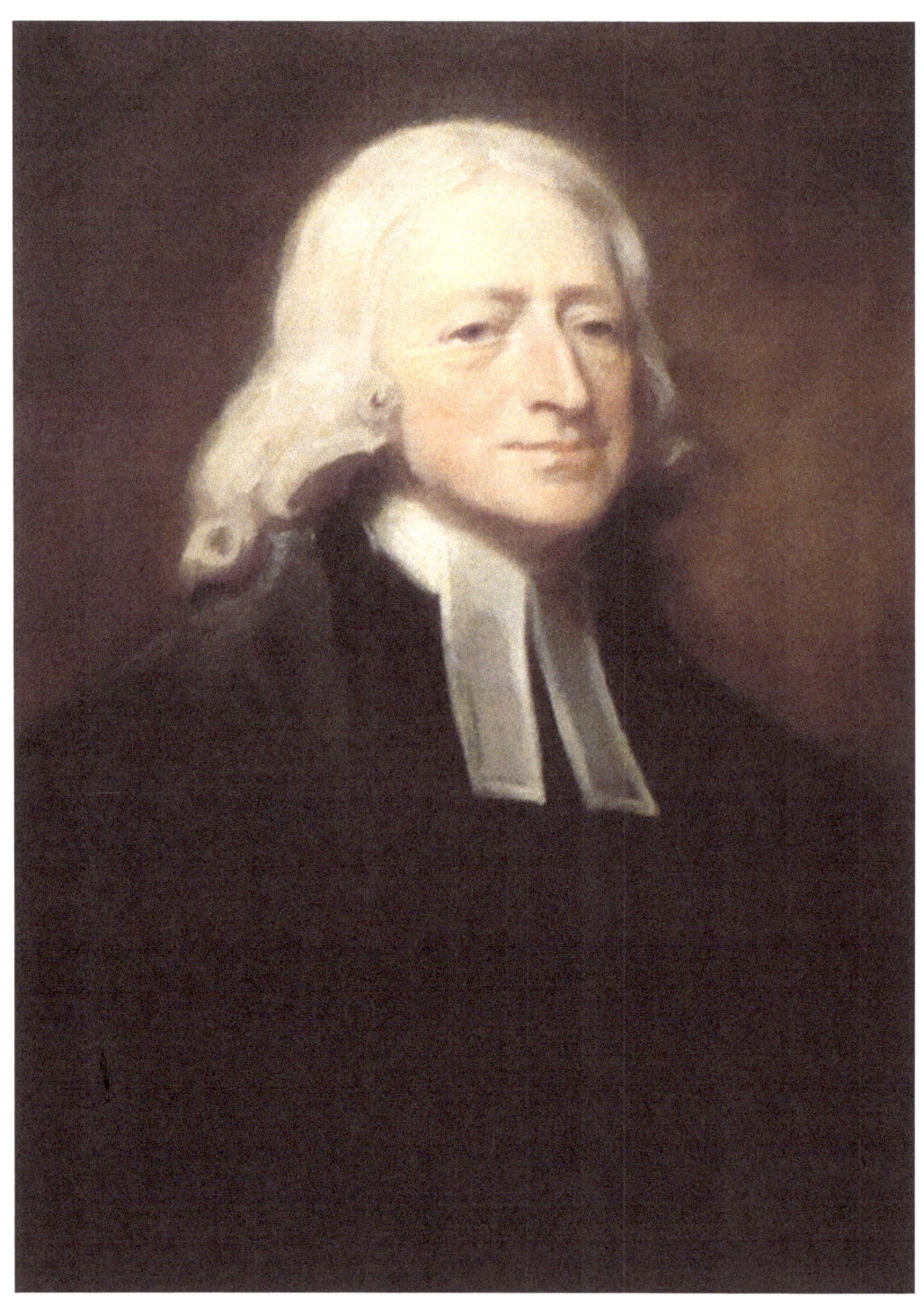

John Wesley, by George Romney (1789)

Wesley the Notable Person

*O*ne of the most prolific portrait painters of the day, in London, was George Romney, who painted representations of many of the great people of the time. The custom of many portraitists was to have style books with choices of pose and type for the customer.[40] In the case of Wesley's portrait by Romney, arrangements were apparently made by Mrs. Tighe, of Ireland, for him to paint Wesley at the end of 1788. Wesley sat for the painter four times over a period of three weeks, taking over ten of his well-guarded hours. Wesley's own evaluation at the time, according to his *Journal*, is that it was *"an exact likeness."*

The painted portrait was finished by February 7, 1789,[41] when Wesley wrote to Mrs. Tighe that it was available. He suggested to her that some of his friends thought it "to be *a good likeness*" and desired engravings of it. He also suggested to her that he could arrange to have the work done...if she would pay for it. The engraver, Jonathan Spilsbury, paid Romney thirty pounds for the portrait and frame, and proceeded to produce a mezzotint.[42] These fairly accurate reproductions Wesley took with him and distributed as gifts to his friends. Mary Clarke, for one, thanked Wesley profusely, but told her friend the next day that, although grateful for the gift, she thought it did not bear

---

40. This process, known to have been used by Reynolds, may account, to some degree, for certain characteristics in some paintings, and perhaps for similarities between paintings of different individuals, such as Forsaith's observation that the nature of the Romney painting of Wesley bears a close resemblance to the portrait of John Henderson, who was a current actor at the time, well-known for playing Falstaff. Forsaith, "The Romney Portrait of John Wesley." *Methodist History* 47 (Part 4, July 2004): 251; Pointon, 41.

41. The painting was later sold by Mrs. Tighe's executors and eventually was acquired by the Museum of Art in Philadelphia, Pennsylvania.

42. Spilsbury's daughter reproduced the Romney-type image, as done by her father, when she created a painting in the mid-nineteenth century depicting Wesley preaching in Ireland at the time of his visit to Mrs. Tighe's in 1790 to deliver the prints.

a strong resemblance to him and was "by no means a striking likeness."[43]

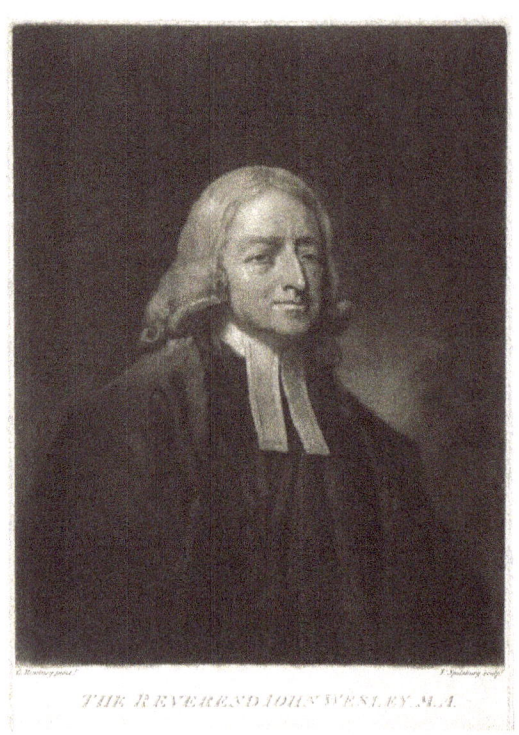

THE REVEREND JOHN WESLEY M.A.

Spilsbury's mezzotint based on Romney

The Romney portrait became a favorite of many—perhaps because of its association with a famous artist, perhaps because of Wesley's published comments about it being "an exact likeness," or perhaps because of the serenity exuding from the painting itself. It also was typical of the "notable person" portraits that did not involve a special context with scholarly books or a preaching or teaching pose. Romney himself made several copies of the Wesley portrait, some of which still exist. If Mary Clarke is correct, however, the favorable evaluations of the painting bore no relationship to its success or failure in reproducing the actual image of Wesley's face. Nevertheless, several painted, lithographed, and engraved copies have been made and adored over the years, some of them even including a fur lining to Wesley's preaching gown, showing more imagination than knowledge of the subject of the painting on the copyist's part.[44]

43. Mrs. Richard Smith, *Mrs. Adam Clarke: Her Character and Correspondence, by her daughter* (London: Partridge & Oakey, 1851), p. 76 (Aug. 11, 1789).

44. There are later painted copies at the National Portrait Gallery, London; Christ Church, Oxford; Lincoln College, Oxford; Wesley's Chapel, London; Wesley's House, London; the New Room, Bristol; the World Methodist Museum, Lake Junaluska; and the Oxford Centre for Methodism and Church History at Oxford Brookes University, to mention a few.

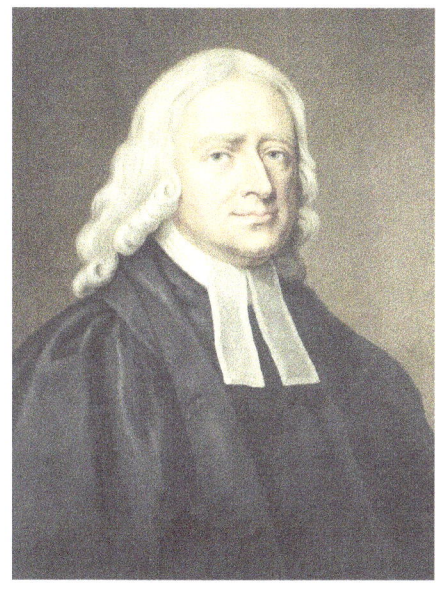

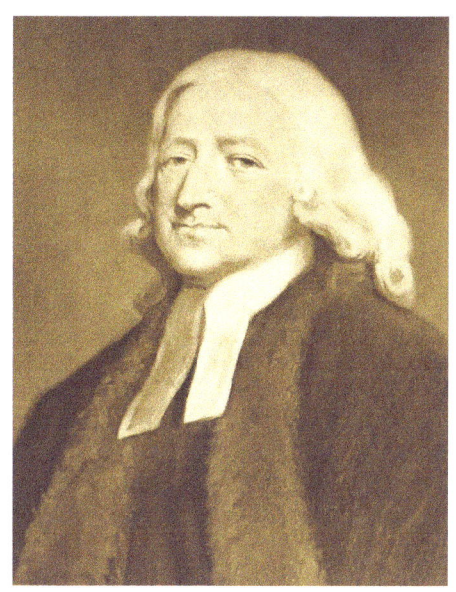

Later color engraving

Engraving of the "fur" portrait, Romney

Miniature by Grimaldi based on Romney

Copy by Romney himself

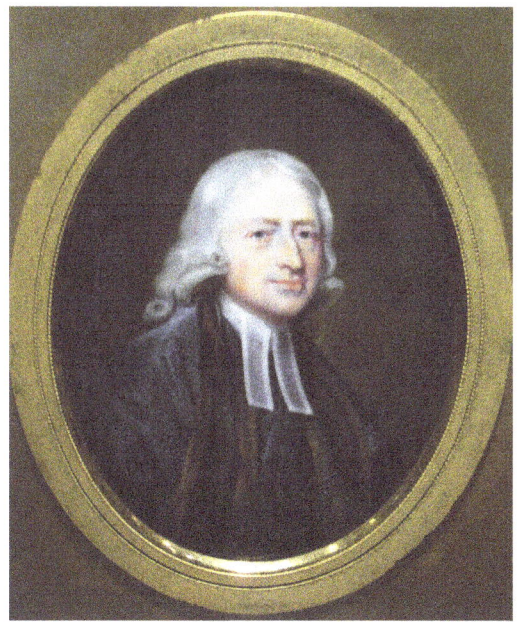

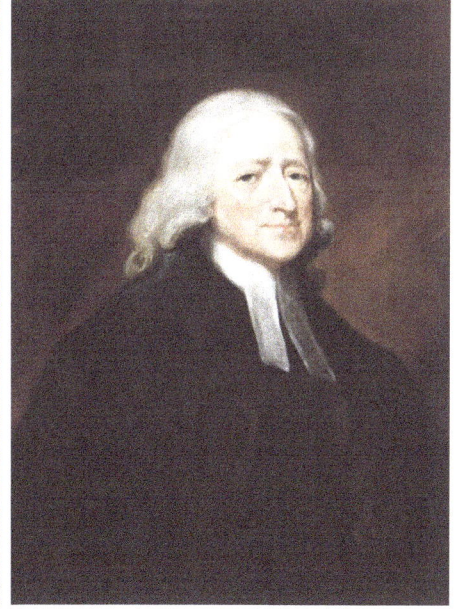

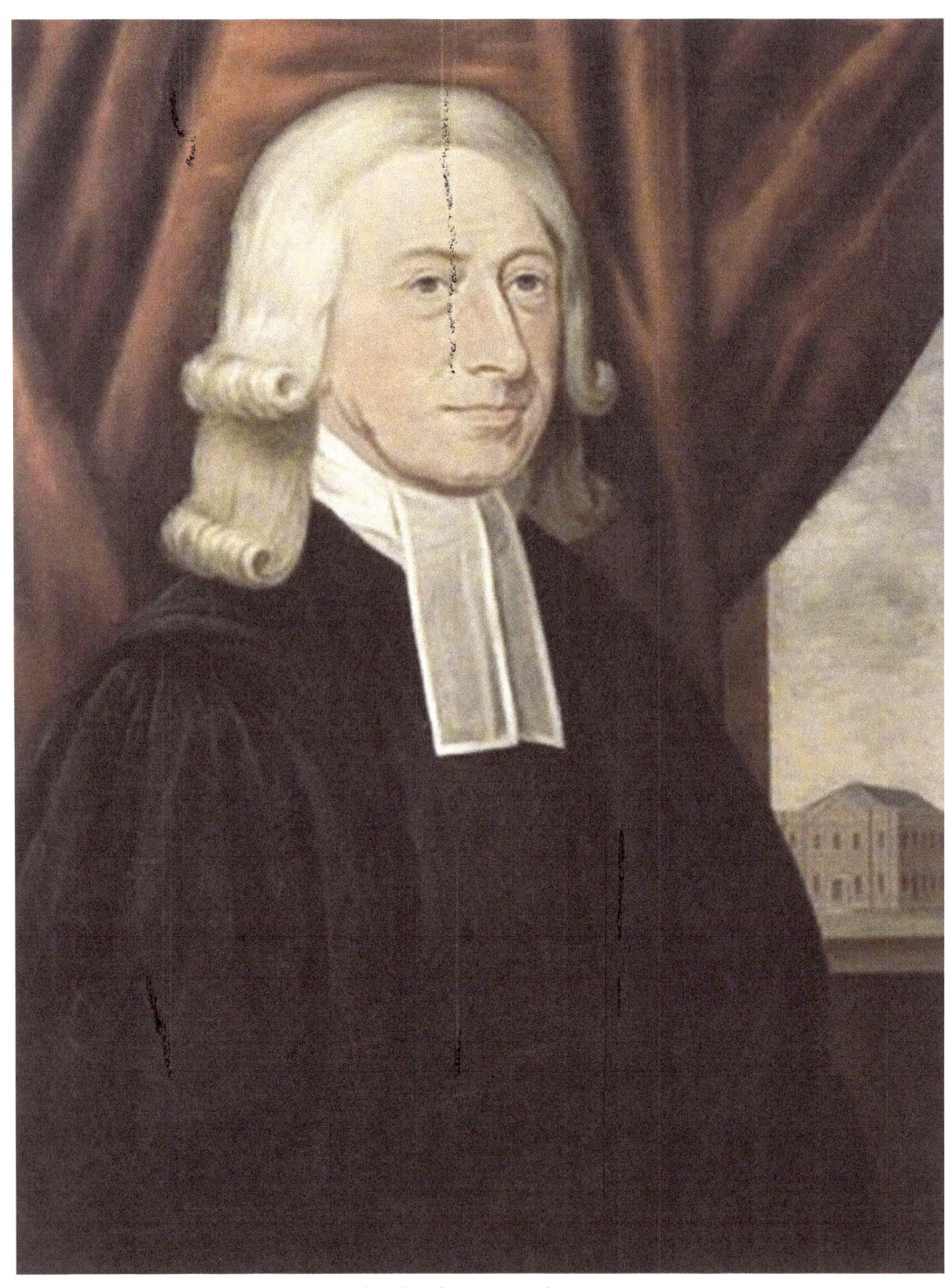

John Wesley, by Thomas Horsley (1784–90?)

Wesley the Notable Methodist

*O*ne of the last portrait paintings of Wesley done from life, depending upon when you date the work, was apparently done by Thomas Horsley in Sunderland in 1784 or 1790, while Wesley was visiting the home of Mr. Lipton, in Wearmouth, or in 1785 when visiting friends in Deptford.[45] Supposedly, his host in Sunderland in 1784 prevailed upon Wesley to sit for his portrait, whereupon Thomas Horsley painted this somewhat stilted picture of an expressionless man with a rather fake-looking wig. The painting was copied by the artist's father, and the original, after remaining in the artist's family for years, was presented to Richmond College in Surrey.[46] The first edition apparently did not have City Road Chapel in the background. The dating is somewhat conjectural.

The second edition, with the Chapel but not yet the elaborate red drape, is listed by John Telford as another painting, though nearly identical, with purported place of origin and the name of the owner presented in the title—the "Deptford-Cummins" portrait. That version of the painting has been shown hanging in Charles Wesley's house in Bristol, though it is sometimes said to have been in Australia for a while.[47] Why the two paintings are not attributed to the same artist is a mystery. The later copy, with pre-1810 City Road Chapel portrayed at the right side, and dominated by the red drape (as seen to left), is presently housed at the Leysian Mission in London.

---

45. Neither the dates nor the places are close to each other.

46. *Notes and Queries* (3rd series) 7 (April 1, 1865): 256. But see Kerslake, 1:304, which dates the work to June 5, 1784, based on Wesley's diary entry, "3 Necessary business, picture!" Actually, there is also an entry on the previous day, "4 Picture!" that might also relate to this portrait. Wesley notes visiting Wearmouth on June 6. *Works,* 23:488.

47. John Telford (*Sayings and Portraits,* p. 118) refers to this painting as the Dornford-Cummins Portrait, saying that it was done for Josiah Dornford in 1785 when Wesley visited Deptford (near London, nowhere close to Sunderland). The painting eventually went for a period to Australia. For an article that exemplifies the Wesley Historical Society approach to issues surrounding the painting of these three portraits by Horsley (as well as other things), see F. F. Bretherton, "Portrait of John Wesley by Thomas Horsley of Sunderland," in WHS *Proceedings* 23 (No. 2, 1942): 31–36.

Wesley the Notable Scholarly Person

At some unknown date, said by some to be close to 1760 but probably after 1775 since it shows Wesley with a wig, a portrait was produced that is supposedly by Johann Zoffany, R.A. The nature of the portrait could be associated with the scholarly style portraits of the 1740s and 1750s, but it is much closer to the pose of the miniatures of Arnold and Barry of the late 1780s, as are the engravings of it. The painting itself had a patterned drape in the background, with some books and a quill pen on a desk beside a sitting Wesley, hands folded on his lap, the latter differing remarkably from Williams.

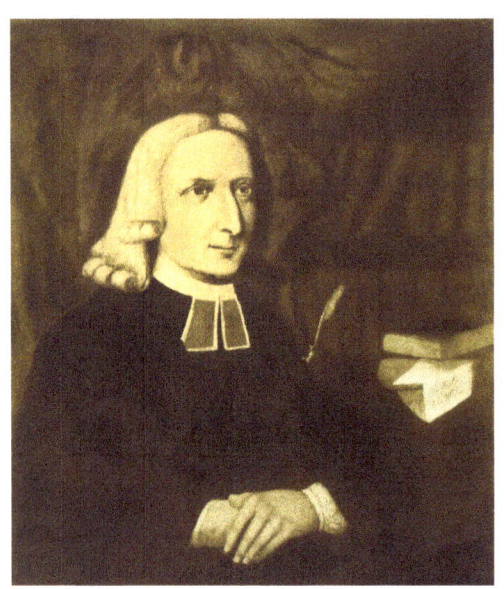

Zoffany/Harding painting of Wesley as scholar, priest, writer, and publisher

This portrait was copied or "delineated" by N. Harding, apparently in the late 1780s, since it was engraved by more than one person in that same period (1788–89) who left out the drapes and books in the background but left the books, quill pen, and note on the desk. Francesco Bartolozzi, R.A., was one of the engravers and William Nelson Gardiner was another. In case the viewer cannot figure out who is portrayed in this painting, the slip of paper between the books gives the inscription, "The Revd John Wesley."

The extant copies of the painting are rather primitive, and the engraved portraits rather strange in the freedoms they take, especially in portraying the hair, the eyes, and the nose. But they do exhibit a resurgence of the "academic image" of Wesley, associated with books, both in the foreground and background.

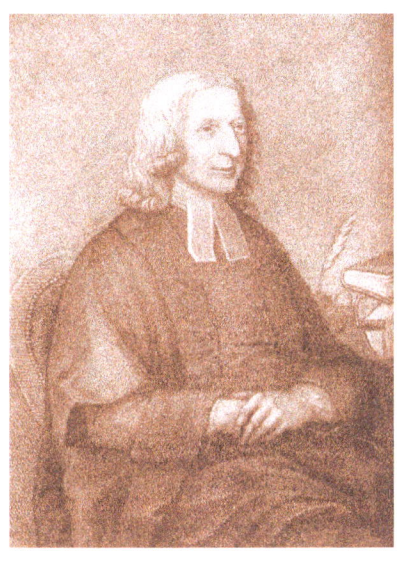

Engraved by Bartolozzi after Zoffany, sometimes printed in red-orange ink

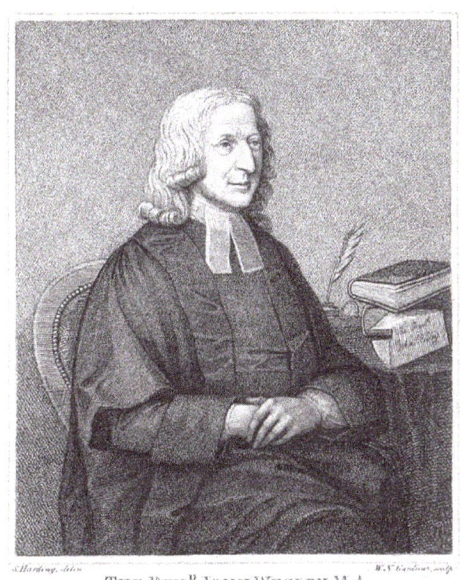

THE REV.ᴰ JOHN WESLEY, M.A.
Aged 85.

Engraved by William Nelson Gardiner after Harding

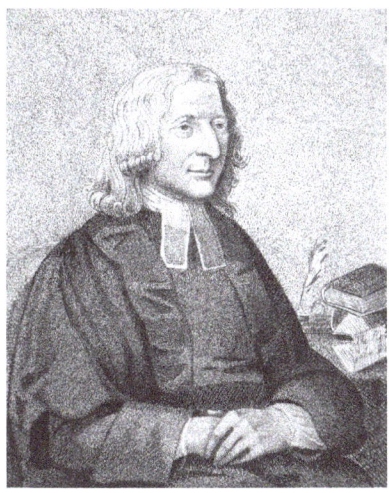

Engraved by S.G., different folds in material, curls in hair, chair details

Detail of Zoffany showing paper with Wesley's name

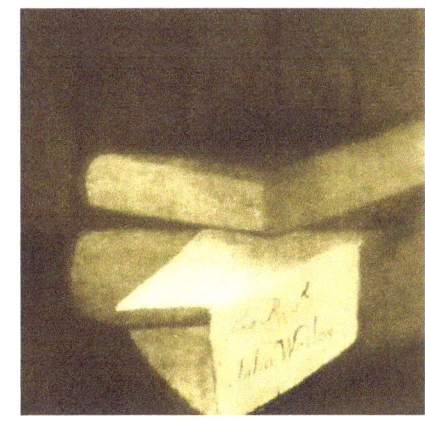

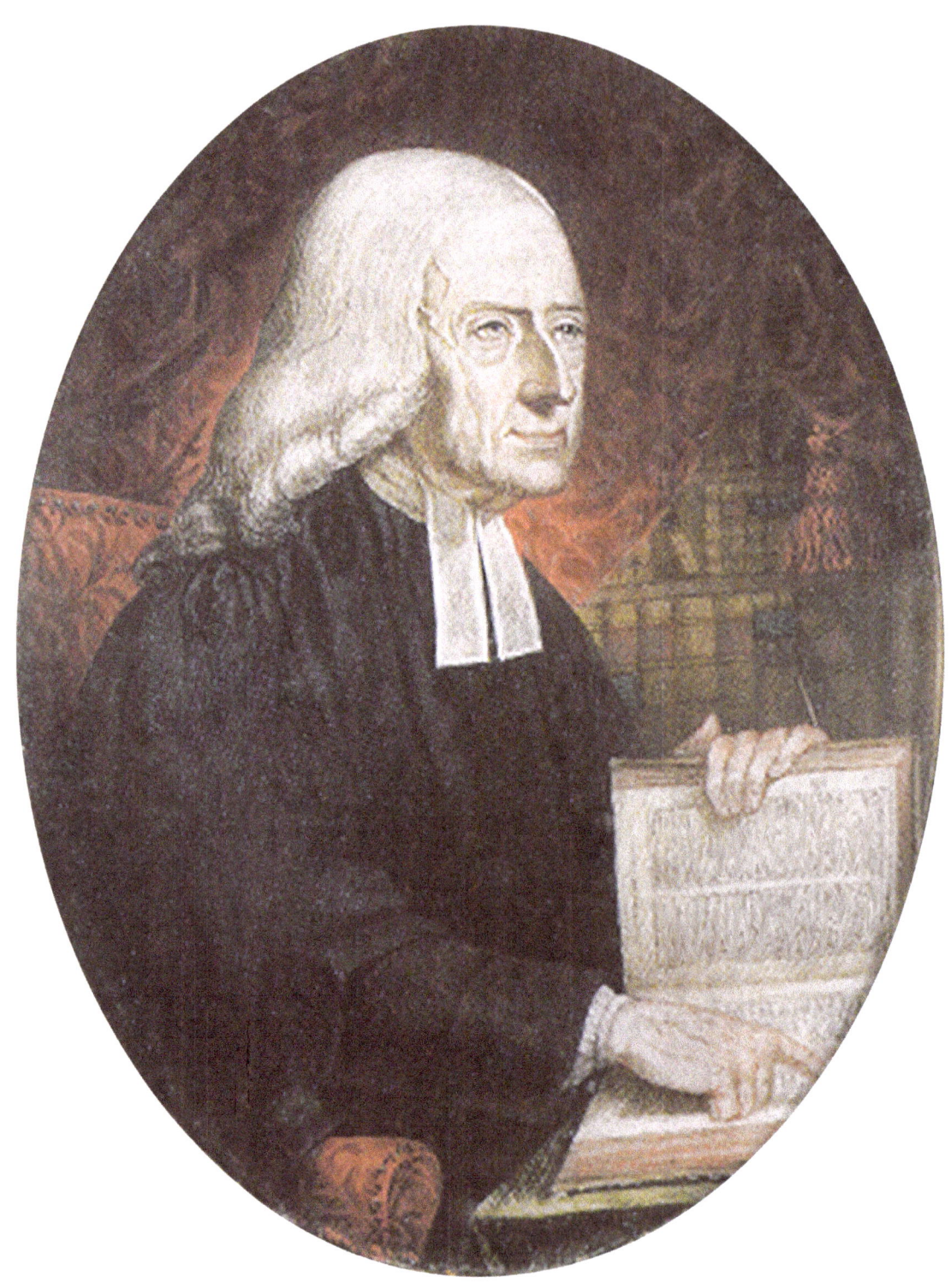

R. Arnold miniature of Wesley (1790)

Wesley the Aging Methodist Leader

A more attractive attempt at portraying the Methodist leader, using much the same pose and background, was accomplished by Robert (or Reginald Edward) Arnold, the miniaturist, in February 1790.[48] Once again, the artist reverts back to the academic image of Wesley as seen in the Williams portrait, with Wesley surrounded by books and reading a large tome, presumably the Bible, given the nature of the type blocks. The red drape is a common attribute in paintings of the day and may indicate quality, as is evident in the nature of the upholstery on the chair and the size of the books on the shelves. Wesley's age is demonstrated by the face, which portrays wrinkles, veins, jowls, and general tiredness, which together give the rather realistic impression of a person in his late eighties. In combination with the Bible, the impression is one of wisdom, piety, and calmness that comes with experience.

This portrait became a favorite, copied by various engravers, such as William Ridley and P. Maguire, partly because it was obviously the portrait of an old man—it certainly was true to life in that sense. This painting, both the pose and face, became the model for many other painters and engravers in the period.

---

48. Kerslake has the original by Barry ("Portrait of a Clergyman," exhibited at the RA in 1790) and the copy by Arnold (1:304), but many have Arnold as preceding Barry. The more familiar process was for the complicated background (as in Arnold's work) to be omitted by the copyist, rather than added. Wesley's diary has him visiting a painter in February 1790. *Works*, 23:166—"I submitted to importunity and once more sat for my picture. I could scarce believe myself! The picture of one in his eighty-seventh year!"

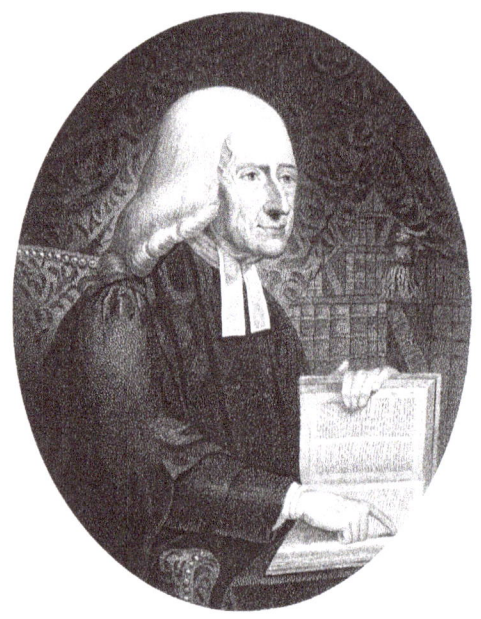 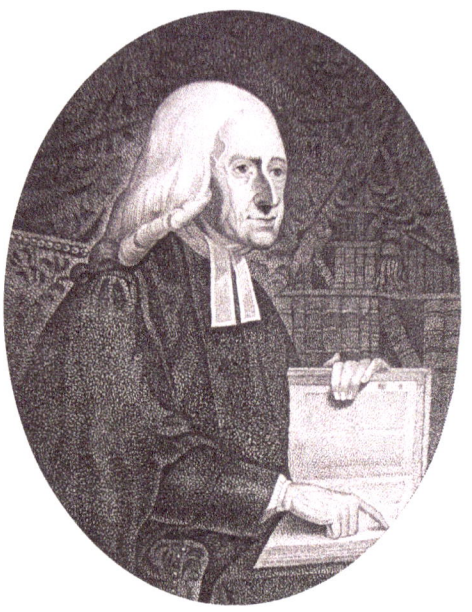

Engraved by Ridley after Arnold (quite a bit later) and sold by John Jones, agent of the Methodists after 1809.

The same plate was re-engraved by P. Maguire (notice the differences in fabric design) and printed even later.

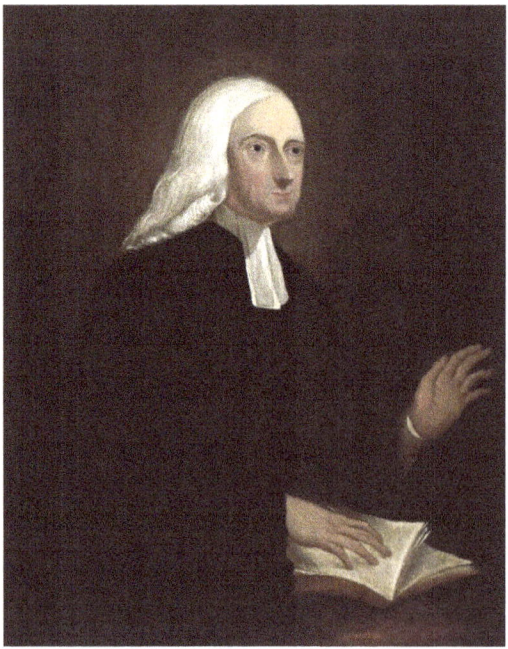

This painting at City Road Chapel, purportedly by James Barry, is a painting of Wesley, recognized by the hair, the prominent nose, and the presence of Geneva tabs. The left hand with palm inside, raised over the Bible held open by the right hand, is not a typical way of portraying Wesley preaching.

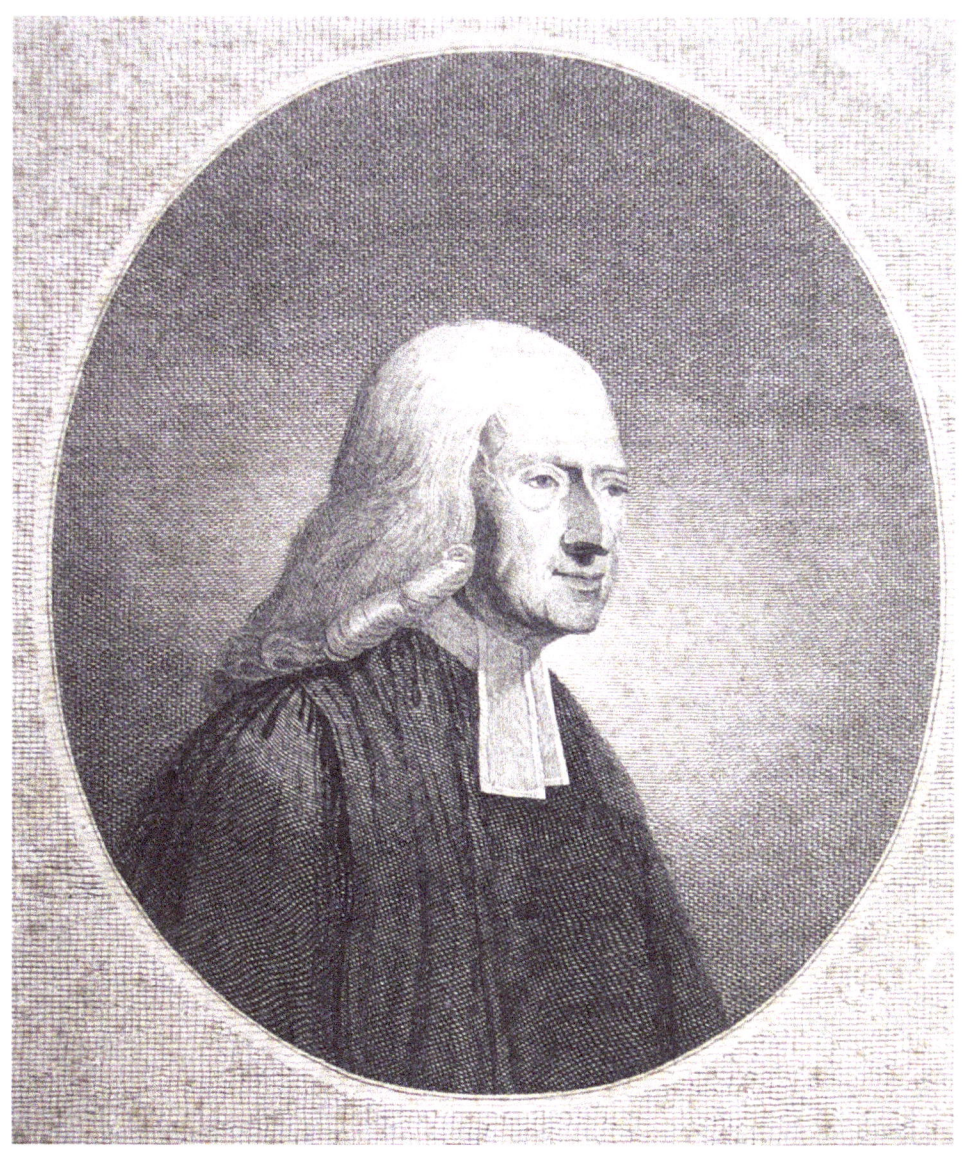

James Barry, R.A., also did a copy of the Arnold face, also
a miniature painting but without the background of books and
drapes, giving credence to it being a derivitive of the Arnold
portrait—the Barry version and its engraved reproductions leave
out details in the background, just as the later copies of Zoffany
leave out the background details.

It seems that the painted portrait supposedly done "shortly
before Wesley's death," purportedly by Benjamin West, R.A.,

was not actually an original by West,[49] but was also based on the Arnold/Barry model, the face especially being an almost exact copy of that visage in the Arnold/Barry mode. The "West" painting differs from the City Road painting by Barry in the position of the right hand and the Bible. This portrait, which has been copied many times over the years, also has been called the "Hitt" portrait and at times has also been seen as the supposed lost portrait by Joshua Reynolds. The attribution to Reynolds and West can be likened to biblical attributions that cite famous authors in order to promote authenticity and status.

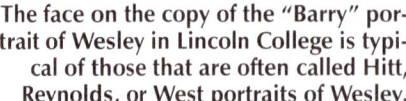

One of the many copies of the "West" portrait.

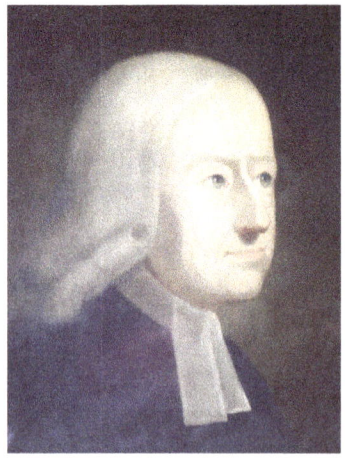

The face on the copy of the "Barry" portrait of Wesley in Lincoln College is typical of those that are often called Hitt, Reynolds, or West portraits of Wesley.

49. The painting is inscribed "BW 1789." Kerslake (1:304) claims it is falsely ascribed to West. If this painting is based on the Barry model, this dating would give credence to Barry having copied Arnold as early as sometime in 1789.

One might say that some of the portraits, such as these, are similar only because they portray the same person, whose image remains the same. That argument would be sound if the other paintings and etchings of the same period portrayed a similar image also. But such is not the case. The variety of visages can easily be divided into groups that are similar to each other—the same angle, the same colors, the same pose, the same visage, the same details, with only slight variations—while the groups themselves show a great deal of variety in their basic image of the man. In evaluating the various groupings of portraits there is no consensus as to how Wesley actually appeared. He was somewhat averse to posing for pictures and did not want to spend the time necessary for the painter to do a decent job. Therefore many of the reproductions of his portrait are copies from other portrayals, which are copies of other attempts to portray the man. The main interest of the painter or particularly the engraver is to make money, not to present an accurate image of the person. Wesley is not alone in this regard. There were no photographs of persons at this period, and the public was presented simply with the efforts of artists, craftsmen, and hacks who were out to make a living by their trade. The name Wesley was mainly what they were selling.

The examples on these recent pages point out some of the ways in which the academic, preaching, and notable person modes of portraits begin to meld together in the Wesleyan iconographic tradition toward the end of Wesley's life. The portraits do not always combine all the types, but the combination of scholarly and preaching attributes becomes especially evident, and he is seldom seen as a ranting revivalist. By the time he is an older man, he is no longer associated with the University but still refers to himself as "Late Fellow of Lincoln College." He is no longer preaching outdoors, but still typically preaches three to five times a day to the Methodist societies. Above all, he has become a truly notable person, one of the most recognizable on the British scene, and that seems to tie together his legacy in all its variant meanings.

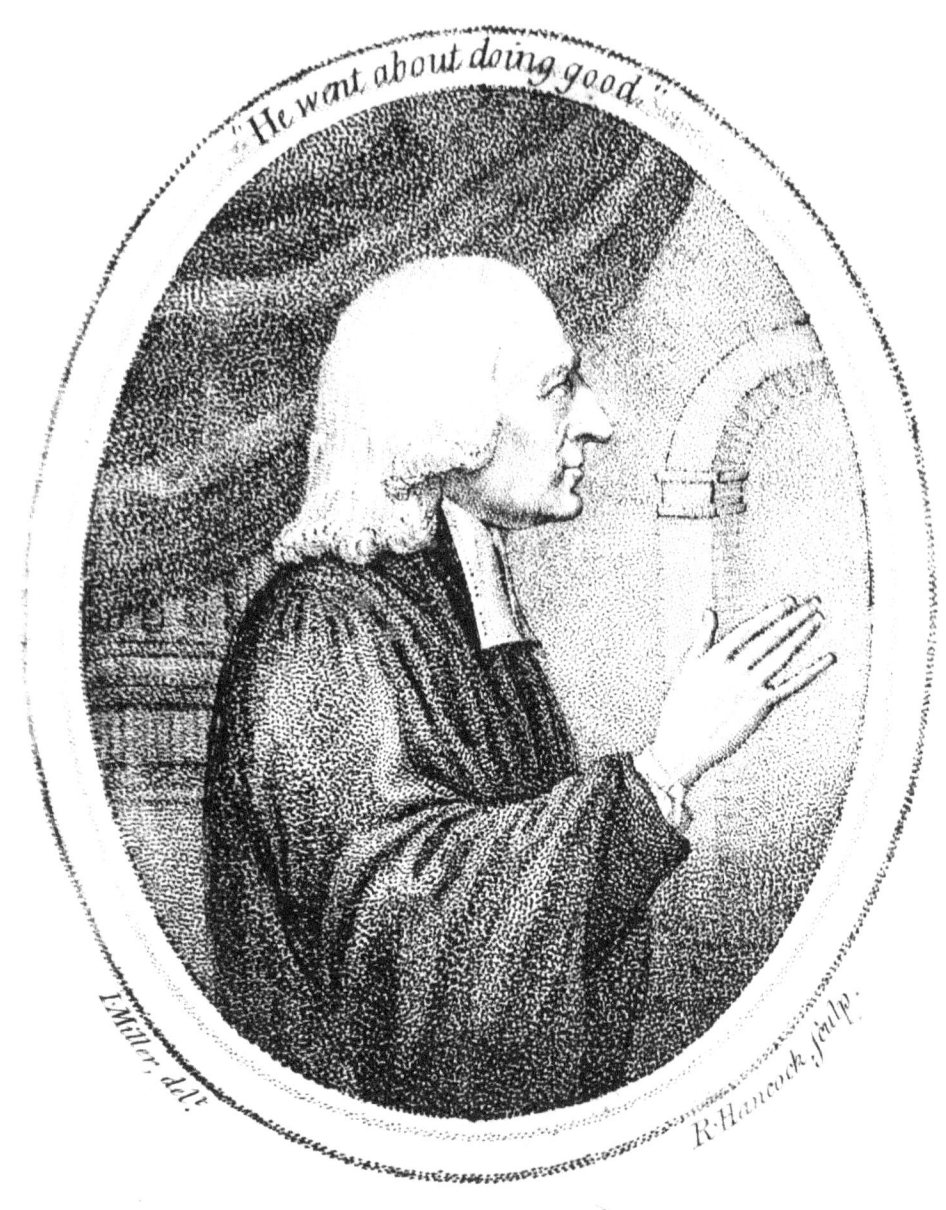

"He went about doing good."

I. Miller delt.

R. Hancock Sculp.

Rev. John Wesley A.M.

London, pub. 1.st Dec.r 1790, by H. Humphry, Old Bond Street.

This stipple engraving is from a 1790 design by James Miller (active 1760–95) and was engraved by Robert Hancock (1783–1817), who had worked for the Staffordshire potteries in the 1770s but seems to have lived in Bristol by this time. The print was published by Miss Hannah Humphrey (c. 1745–1818), who started out publishing in the 1780s with her brother William but had recently taken over the business and had moved from New Bond Street to No. 18 Old Bond Street.

The design is a profile three-quarters portrait in a preaching pose, with library shelves filled with books and a drape in the background. An unusual feature is the arched doorway in the wall behind the raised right hand, palm facing inward. The face could be similar to other profiles that were beginning to be done, but the similarity could also be the result of actually knowing the approximate appearance of the subject, who was famous by the time the print came out in December 1790, when he was eighty-seven years old, just about three months before he died.

The importance of the print is not only the somewhat pleasing appearance of the subject, but also the combination of the "preaching" style of portrait and the "academic" setting with the books, a clear tendency in the portrayals of Wesley in his later life. These features, as well as the stone archway in the right background, are not typical of a Methodist preaching house.

And one wonders if the separation of the pinkie finger in the raised hand is typical of Wesley's preaching style. Most of the portrait is probably, in this and other cases, the result of the fixtures in the studio or in the artist's imagination. The artistic balance that is characteristic in this engraving would not be evident in most Wesleyan preaching settings.

The visage itself, therefore, is probably the result of the artist's conception of the man, copying, with some variation, his image from other portrayals that were available at the time—especially the nose, the hair and the Geneva bands—combined with any general view that the artist thinks is appropriate to his image of the man.

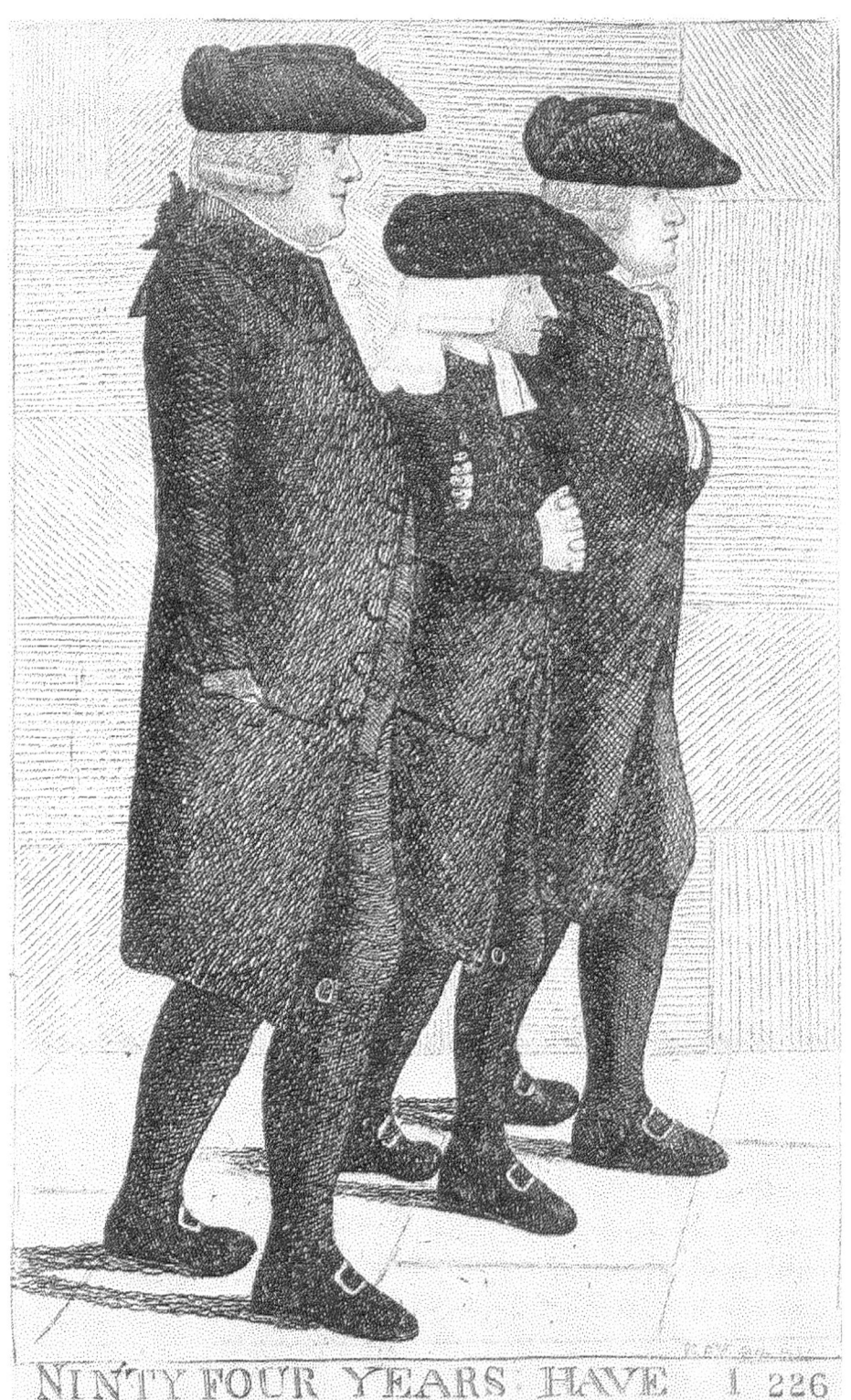

NINTY FOUR YEARS HAVE I 226
SOJOURNED UPON THIS EARTH
ENDEAVOURING TO DO GOOD

The John Butterworth Jr., silhouette, in black paper, is said to be one of the last likenesses of the Methodist leader taken from life. It was done on May 1, 1790, when Wesley visited Leeds on his way to the annual Conference in Scotland. The inscription was added after Wesley's death ten months later.

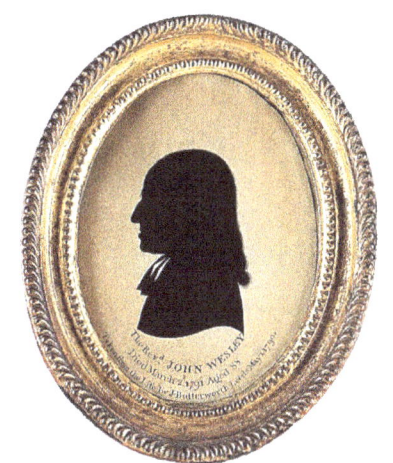

The often copied portrait of Wesley walking with two friends in the streets of Edinburgh (opposite) was done while Wesley was there in mid-May 1790. The artist was John Kay, a prolific Scottish engraver who, according to legends on subsequent printings of the scene, sketched them hurriedly as they passed by his place when Wesley was in town for the Conference, which was, as it turned out, his last visit. The caption, which purports to quote Wesley, is incorrect in the details, obviously, since Wesley was only eighty-seven during his last year.[50] Later printings change the quotation to "eighty seven years" and identify the other persons as James Hamilton, M.D., and James Cole, who was a Methodist minister stationed in Edinburgh at the time.

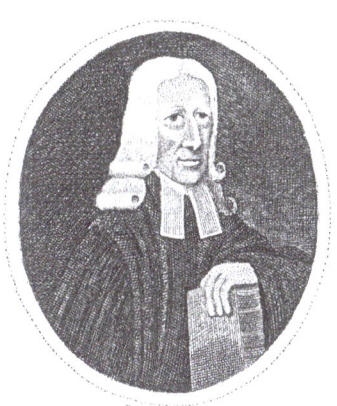

The small engraving by John Kay is also dated the year before Wesley died,[51] but looks more like a caricature than a serious portrayal of the Methodist revivalist. It does show him presumably preaching, with his left hand on a large book, his index finger holding a place that one thinks must be his text, similar to many other preaching portraits. This engraving is one of an amazing series that Kay intended to publish but never did, one that included over nine hundred images of famous people who visited his city.

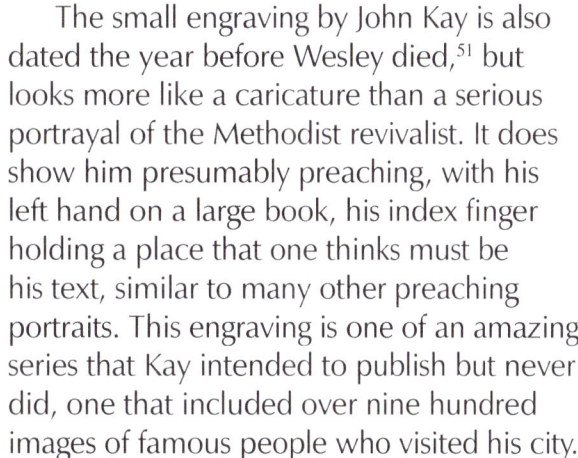

---

50. See the excellent article by Donald Ryan, "The Edinburgh Wesley Portraits," in WHS *Proceedings* 55 (February 2005): 1-13. "Kay fecit 1790" is in the lower right-hand corner, over the volume and page number.

51. In John Kay, *Series of Original Portraits and Caricature Etchings by the Late John Kay, Miniature Painter* (Edinburgh: Paton, Carver, and Gilder, 1837).

Wesley in Death

*J*ohn Wesley died on March 2, 1791, after a one-week illness, about four months before his eighty-eighth birthday. The death mask (plaster cast) that was taken from his face is a check against the variety of portraits of him that appeared during his lifetime. The mask shows clearly, besides the flattened eyes from the pennies placed there to keep his eyelids closed, the long pointed nose, which appears in virtually every portrait of him, and the upper right lip bulging from an apparent raised eyetooth, which is never portrayed in the paintings, drawings, etchings, or busts, and a prominent forehead above the eyes.

Ridley, a common engraver of later Wesley portraits, took a

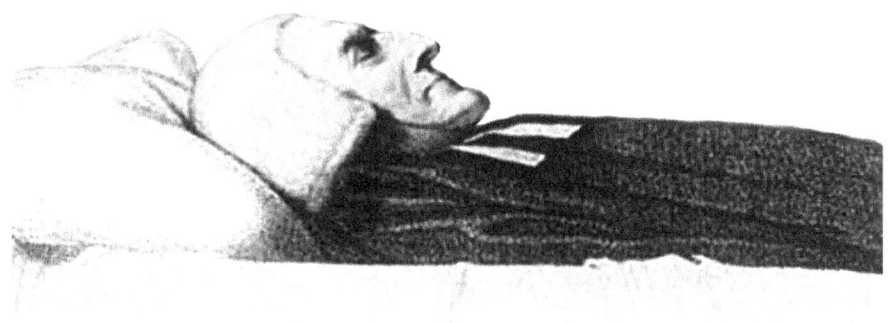

drawing of Wesley lying in state at City Road Chapel before his funeral. It reinforces the three well-known features associated with Wesley and therefore of images of him—a prominent nose, curls at the bottom end of his hair, and Geneva bands with his preaching gown.

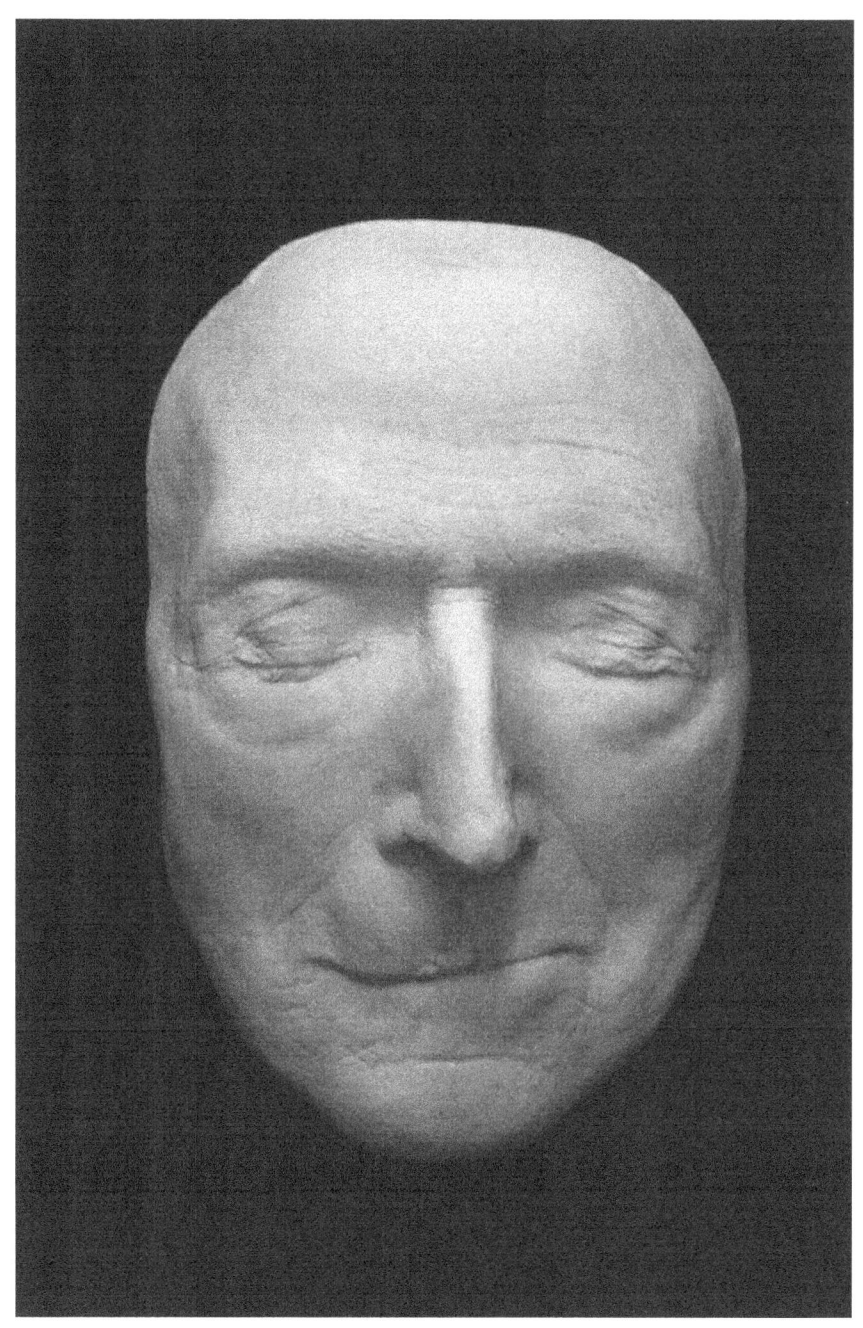

Wesley death mask (1791)

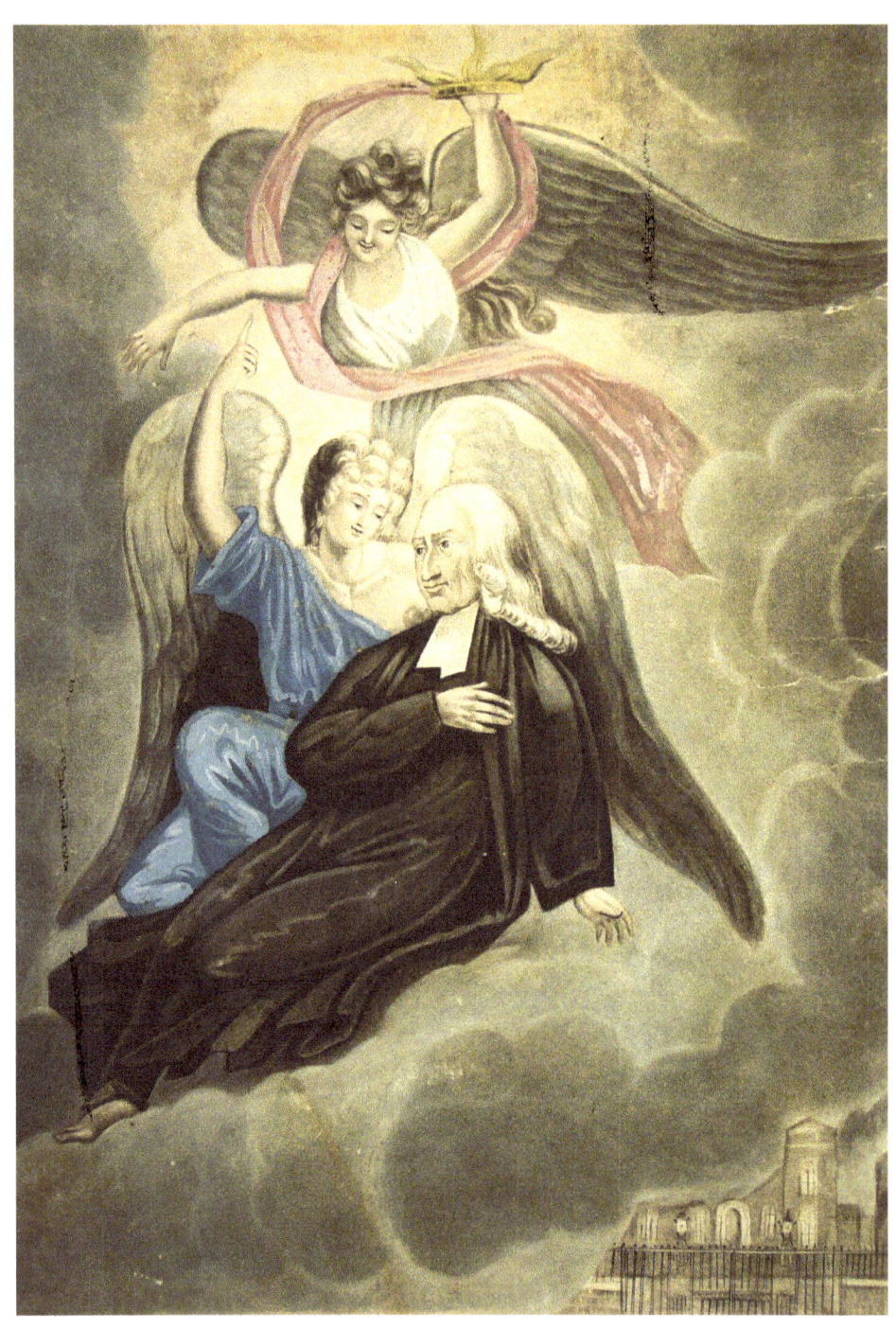

"John Wesley, that Excellent Minister of the Gospel,
Carried by Angels into Abraham's Bosom" (1791)

The Arnold/Barry model of Wesley's face, in particular, became a favorite pattern for picturing the man for years in many forms. At Wesley's death, the funeral biscuit wrapper at City Road contained a tiny portrait that resembles Arnold.

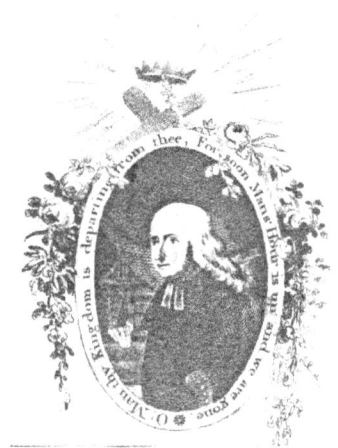

Funeral biscuit cover, March 1791

The somewhat fanciful apotheosis of John Wesley, "Carried by Angels into Abraham's Bosom"—circulated within a month of his death, like it was ready to go—reinforces the frequent pattern of artists simply adapting the Arnold/Barry style of facial features to whatever body position is used in the picture.

The Barry version of the Arnold portrait becomes a favorite of some copyists for generations after Wesley's death.[52]

---

52. See especially W. T. Fry's submission to the Book Committee in 1824, p. 74 below.

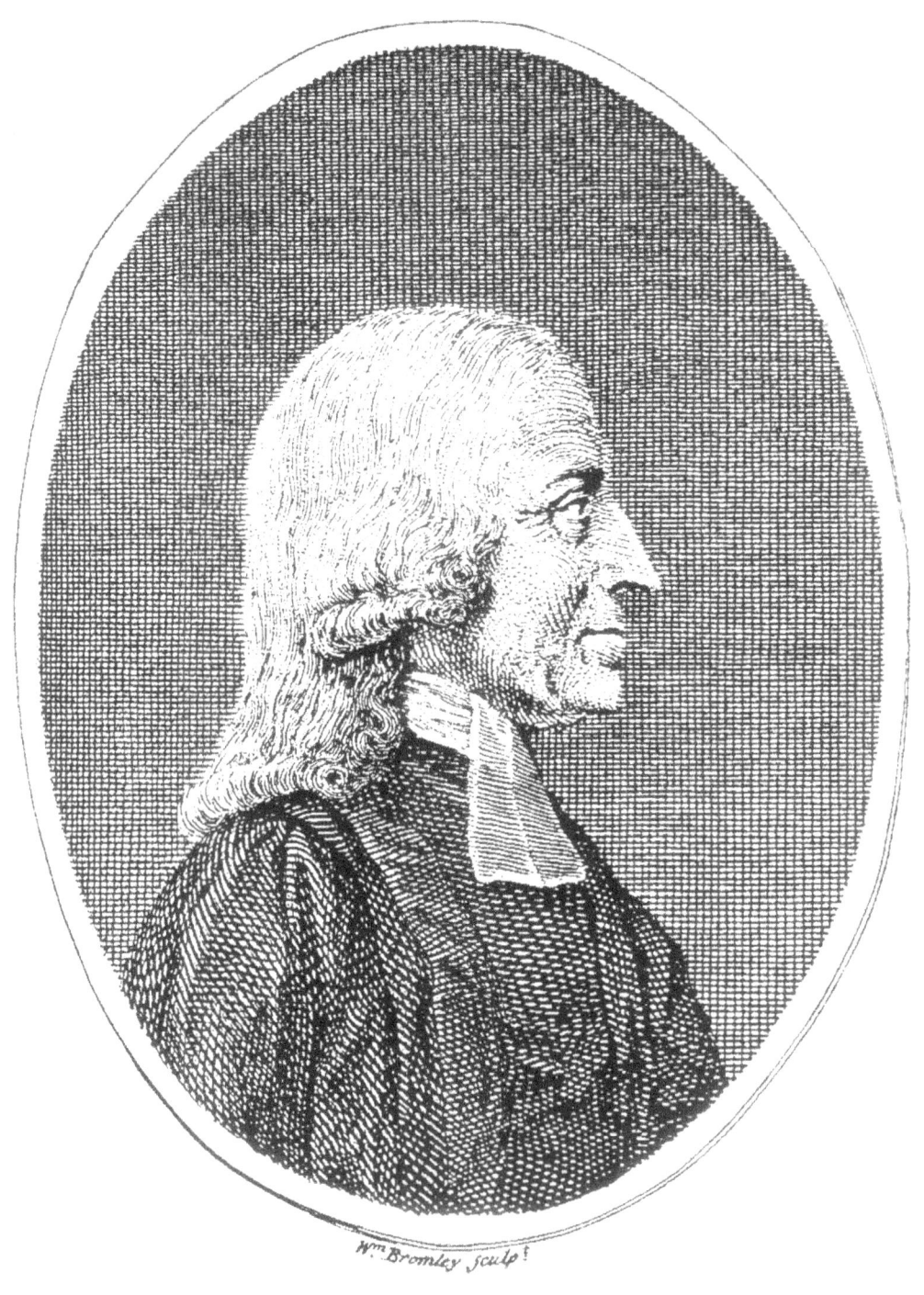

Wm Bromley sculp!

70

Wesley Portrayed Post-Mortem

*O*ne major alternative in the Wesley portraits that appear toward the end of Wesley's life is the profile portrait, such as the miniature by Henry Bone, R.A., and the anonymous frontispiece following it (p. 43). These might anticipate some of the focus on phrenology in the following century.[53] The first major one to appear after Wesley's death, and perhaps the best in some idyllic or iconic ways, was engraved by William Bromley and published in the *European Magazine* less than a month after the end of Wesley's life in 1791.

Closely allied to that style were the portraits by Thomas Holloway (published Apr. 25 and May 24, 1791), which were also profile images, though not as flattering as the Bromley. The first engraving was very much in keeping with its use as the frontispiece to volume one of John Hampson's biography of Wesley, which was not always a flattering literary piece. The second one shows Wesley preaching with a Bible in his left hand, right hand raised with palm down, from a pulpit sporting a velvet cushion, more typical of the Church of England than a Methodist preaching house.

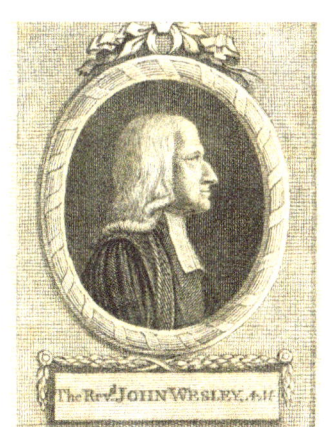 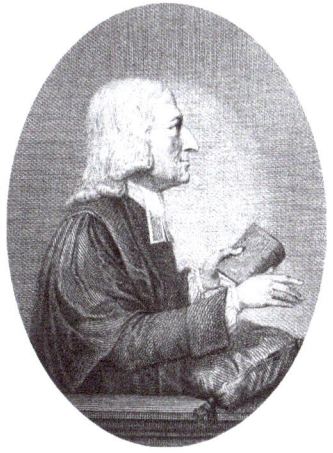

---

53. Suggested by Peter Forsaith. This study of the relationship between skull size and shape and a person's character or mental faculties was begun as a scientific venture by Franz Josef Gall in 1796 and made popular by his associate, Johann Spurzheim, after their meeting in 1800.

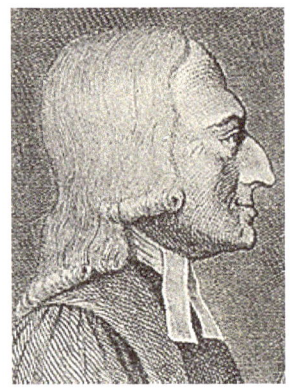

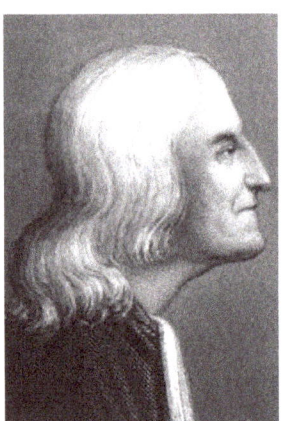

The profile image, practically unused in Wesley portraits prior to his death, became a frequent way of portraying and caricaturing Wesley after his death. The picture at the top left is by N. Nasmyth (1791, here reversed for comparison), and seems to follow very closely the pattern set by Holloway on the previous page. The image below it, purportedly by Thomas Worlidge (1700–66), a member of the Royal Academy, was used later as a frontispiece for a biography of Wesley in the middle of the nineteenth century and is similar in shape and tone to both the Nasmyth, Holloway, and the "Pious Preacher" (see pp. 35–37).

The image of Wesley by Louis Vaslet (fl. 1770–99) was done by the Bath artist either when Wesley visited his home in the late 1780s or later from memory. It was subsequently engraved by John Jones within an oval and published three months after Wesley's death in May 1791. The

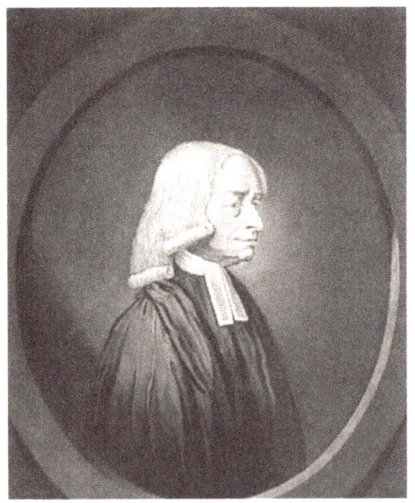

Jones's engraving of Vaslet's drawing (1791)

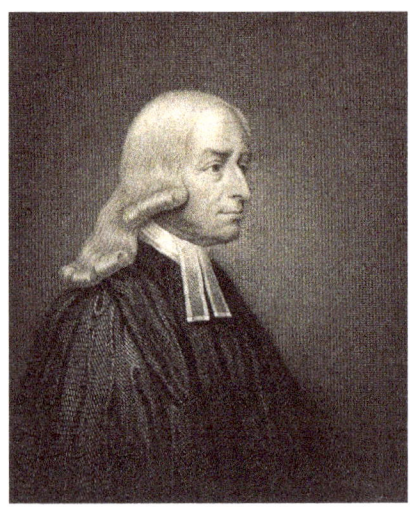

Dean's engraving of Vaslet (1836)

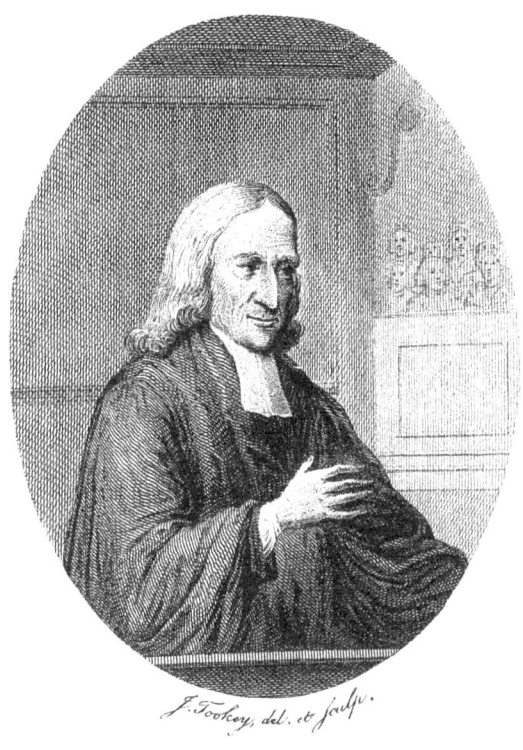

J. Tookey, del. et sculp.

very nice engraving by Thomas Dean was done much later as a frontispiece to Tegg's London edition of volume two of Wesley's *Survey of the Wisdom of God in Creation* (1836).

The portrait of Wesley by J. Tookey was published shortly after Wesley's death and portrays the three typical elements that are present in most of the other portraits—the long nose, curls at the end of long hair, and Geneva tabs. The face is somewhat thin or gaunt and elongated, also not dissimilar from many other later portrayals.

However, this portrait differs from most others, before or after, by having people in a balcony behind Wesley. He is shown in a preaching pose, right hand extended with palm inward and left hand out of sight but apparently resting on the edge of the box pulpit. The location could be a Methodist preaching house, but the sloped ceiling shows it is not City Road Chapel. The cornice that decorates the junction of the internal wall and the ceiling might give a hint as to the place, if it is portrayed accurately.

The post-mortem portraits of Wesley tended to stray further from the actual visage, as evidenced by the increasing variety of images produced as time went on. The actual looks of the man became even less important; even the quality of the print was no longer a selling point. The name was prominently displayed, the connection with Oxford often included, and the calmness of his apparent demeanor belied his early reputation as a controversial revivalist and field preacher. The attacks on his followers diminished noticeably during his later years, but by that time, he had become a somewhat respectable figure of legendary proportions. A fascinating combination of the Arnold and Barry portraits is one executed by the engraver W. T. Fry in 1824 for the Wesleyan Book Committee, which was trying to create an acceptable portrait of Wesley to use as the frontispiece for their hymnal and other publications. Fry's engraving tried to overcome the variety in many eighteenth-century portrayals of Wesley by adopting the Arnold/Barry face and then more or less combining the other features of those two pictures, although in the details they differ greatly from

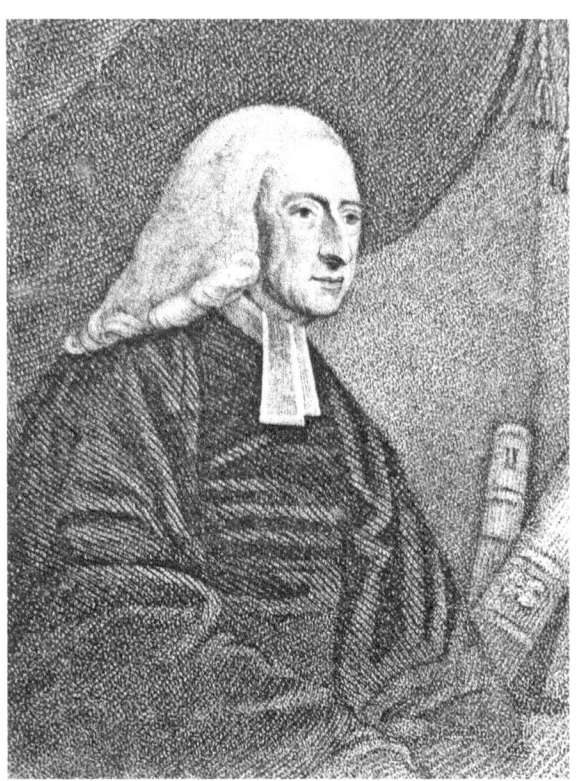

W. T. Fry's entry to the Book Committee for a "standard" portrait of Wesley (1824)

each other and from Fry's efforts. He left off most of the chair, the open Bible, the library shelves with books, and the hands from the Arnold portrait, but added to the Barry concept some background (the red hanging curtain), and included some books that were labeled like the two books found in the early Williams portrait of 1742—perhaps volume two of the Book of Homilies or the *Hymns and Sacred Poems* and a large thick Bible. He produced a strange attempt at synthesis.

The Book Committee eventually passed over Fry's attempt and chose the portrait by John Jackson, R.A., in 1827 (see pp. 84–85).

The variety of preaching poses in the Wesley portraits is further enlarged by the portrait following the Arnold/Barry model that was struck in Philadelphia in the nineteenth century and re-struck over 150 years later. The copperplate (below right), given to Bridwell Library at Southern Methodist University by Frederick Maser, illustrates both this additional pose and the relationship of plate to printed paper. Wesley the preacher has both hands raised over the Bible—one of only a few such examples—and he is preaching from a pulpit within a church, giving the sense of ecclesiastical propriety typical of the Anglican scene (see also the column in the Hamilton portrait).

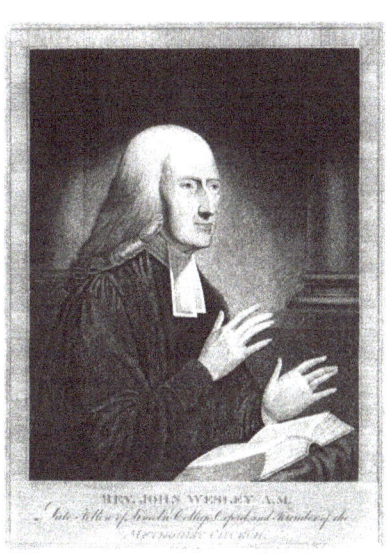
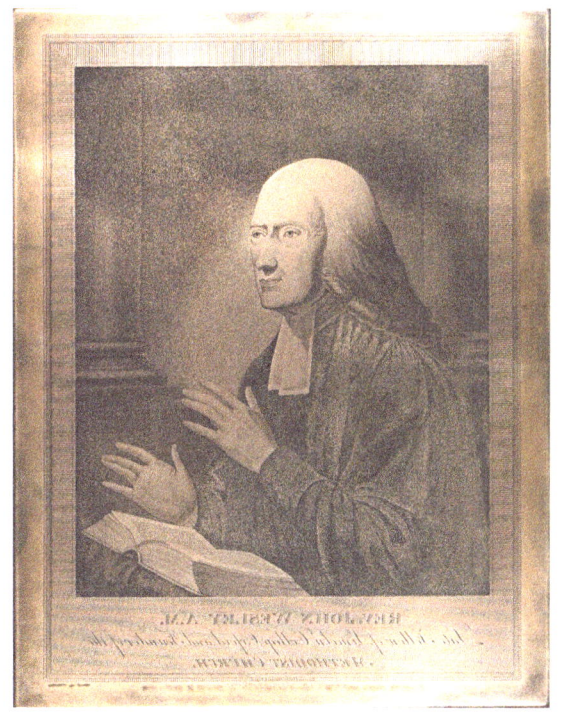

These examples point out some of the ways in which the academic, preaching, and notable-person modes of portraits begin to meld together in the Wesleyan iconographic tradition toward the end of Wesley's life. After his death, Wesley continues to be portrayed in a variety of ways that often combine these features in a manner that the artist finds useful and appropriate to the task as well as to the public's taste.

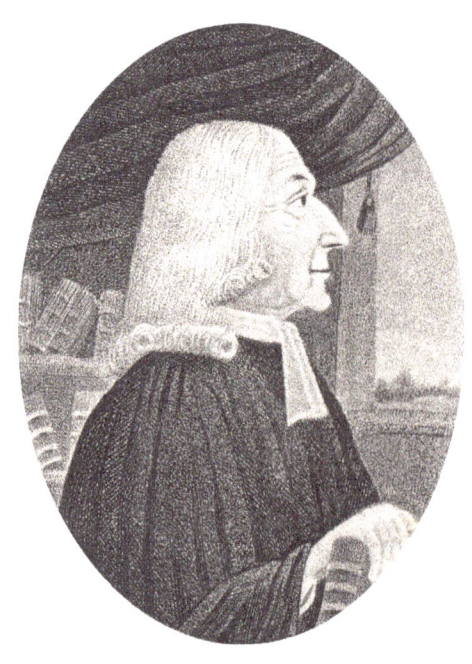

The engraving by L. Palin, also produced after Wesley's death, while seeming to follow the Edridge model of using a profile view with a double row of curled locks on Wesley's wig, is unique in showing him looking through a window, with the landscape in the background, a typical Renaissance ploy. The artist also includes a typical drape in the background, and has the two main features of the "academic" portraits—library books on shelves in the background and Wesley's hand on a book that rests vertically on the invisible table in front of him (see the early Williams portrait).

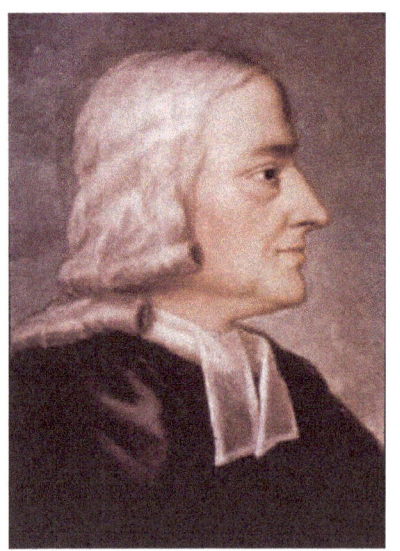

The anonymous "Aristocratic" portrait is typical of some post-mortem portrayals in the sense that the artist seems not to have paid much attention to previous attempts to portray the "real" John Wesley. The angle is straight from the side, typical of the portraits produced in Wesley's later life. But the shape of the head is somewhat more square than many pictures, and the forehead quite prominent—that is to say, the hairline is receding. The artist seems to have incorporated the three basic elements of a portrait of the mature Wesley—the long pointed nose, the long white hair with a double row of curls at the bottom, and the Geneva tabs, though one is turned over. The features are otherwise very clean, giving the portrait its nickname.

76

The round shape of some early portraits gave the shape to many post-mortem medallions that portray some of the traditional engravings of paintings or drawings. The top medallion, undated but rather late, includes an engraving of the first portrait of Wesley, by Williams (reversed). The early portrait of the Williams painting, in its many reproductions, had a long-lasting popularity.

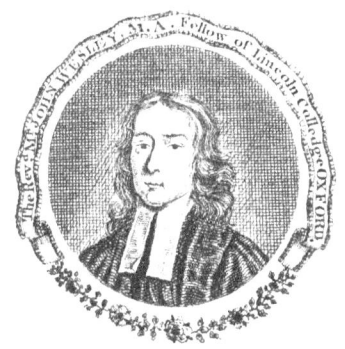

The middle oval uses a version of the Zoffany/Arnold portrayal (reversed) surrounded by the lettering that identifies the subject as Wesley. The year of his death is accurate, but his age at that time was eighty-seven, not eighty-eight—he was in his eighty-eighth year. The medallion simplifies the background by omitting the library shelf full of books, found in many "academic" portraits such as the one by Miller. But it does try to balance the space by putting part of the drape on the left.

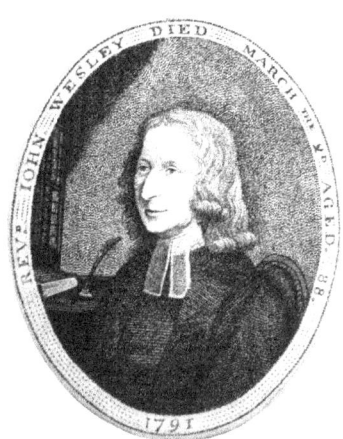

The third example, the Seal of the Methodist Conference of Great Britain, incorporates the bas-relief by John Flaxman that Wedgewood used on the Grecian-ware medallions that his firm produced. The phrase, "What hath God wrought," is from Wesley's writings and refers of course to the extraordinary work that God had wrought in his day by Methodism.[54]

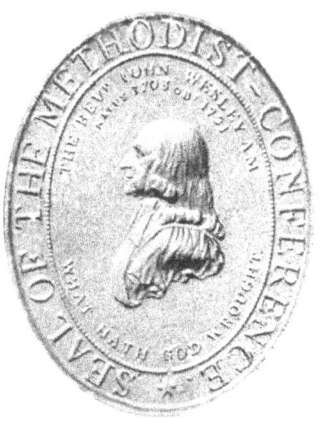

54. See Wesley's explanation of his use of this phrase, in his sermon "On the Laying of the Foundation of the New Chapel," in *Works*, 3:579.

Henry Edridge's profile drawing of Wesley, engraved by Ridley in March 1792, was used as the frontispiece for the Coke and Moore biography of Wesley, a popular, mainline work that sold out of its ten-thousand-copy print run before Conference had met that year. It thus gained wide circulation and became a favorite model for Methodists to copy and imitate for generations to come, whether

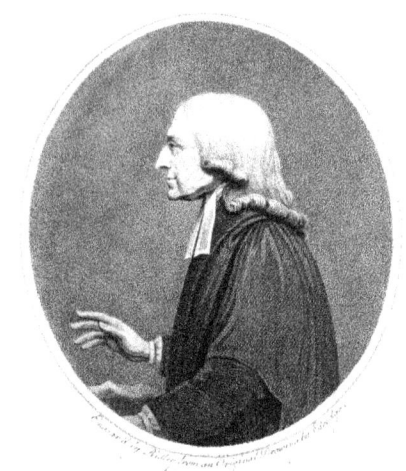

it be for book frontispieces, bas-reliefs, or just illustrations.

Many times the image was bowdlerized: sometimes the preaching pose was lost (the slightly raised hand is missing), the image is reversed, details were somewhat changed or lost in the creation of a woodcut, or the face is much fuller, as with R. Page's later copy (left), which seems to follow the heavier face of the Flaxman and "Roubiliac" ceramics (see p. 42). But the same basic profile preaching image stayed the same—with the mouth always closed.

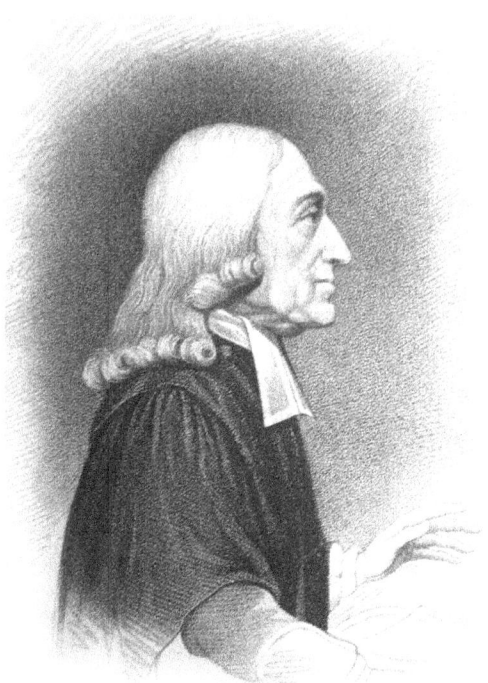

Page's copy of Edridge's engraving (1829)

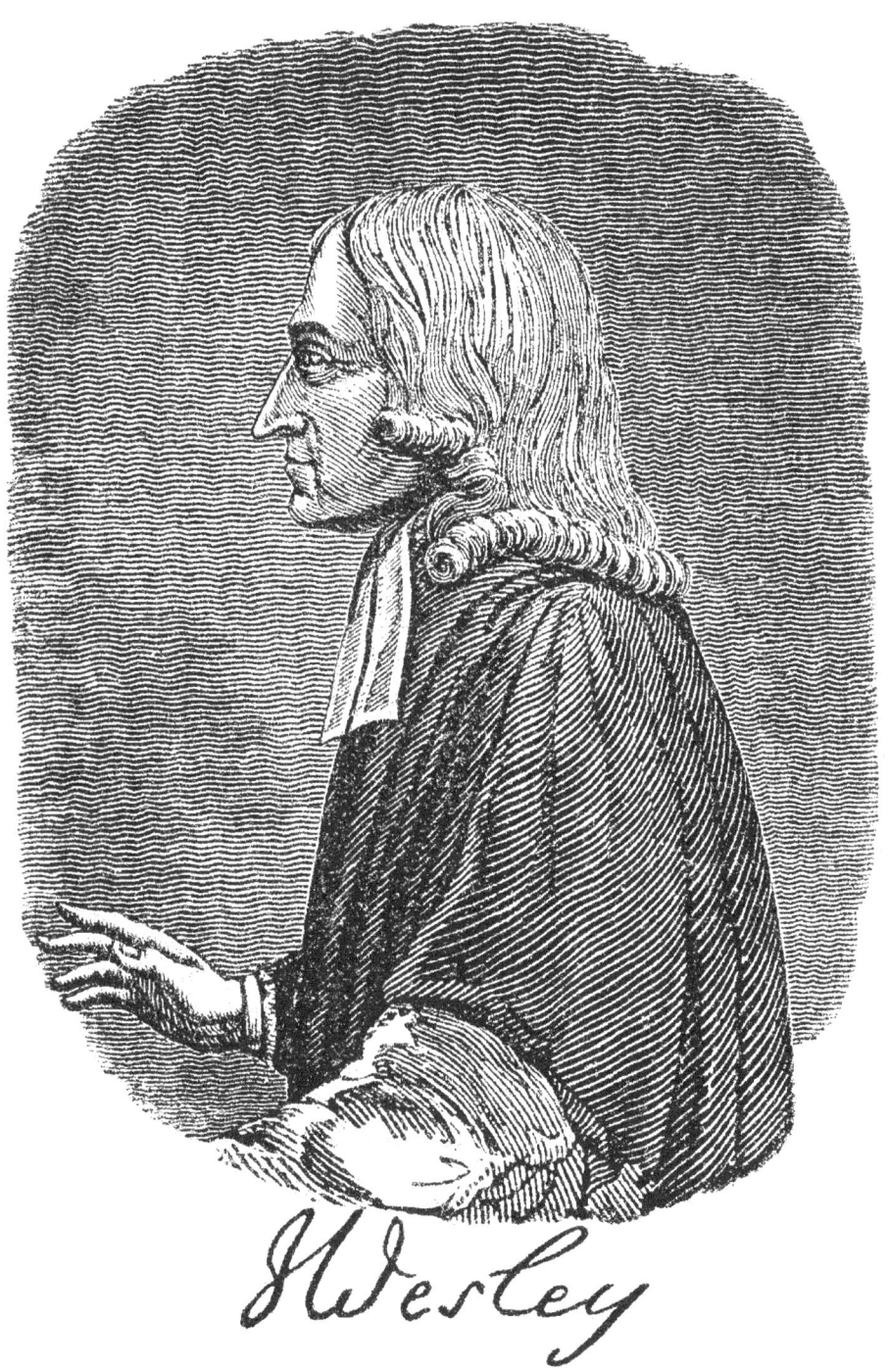

Frontispiece from an American Methodist Episcopal hymnal (1843)

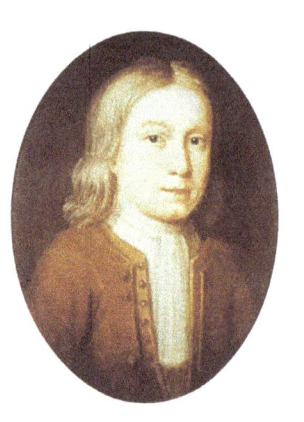

(a) (b)

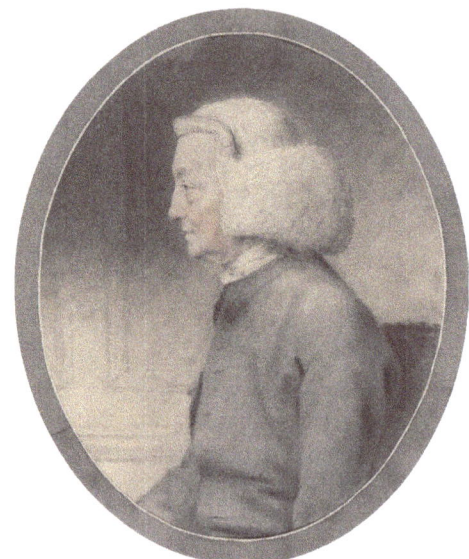

(c)

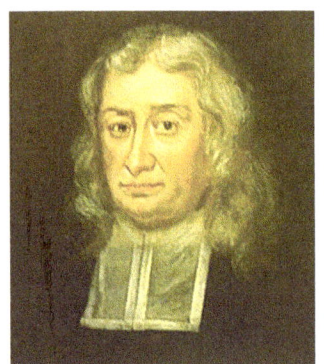

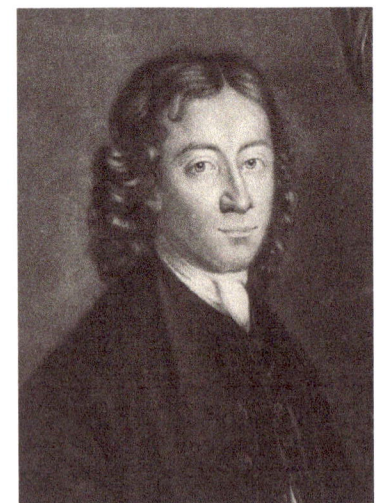

(d) (e)

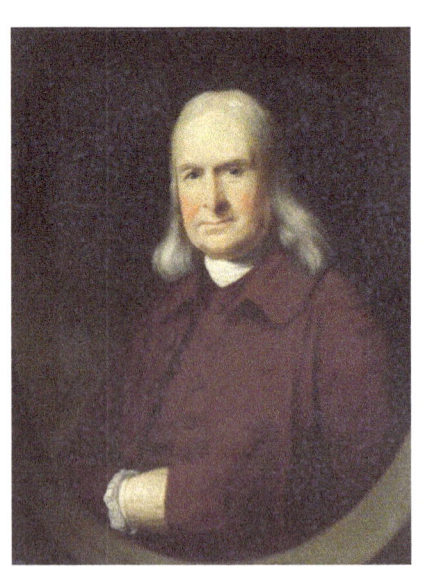

Portraits Purported to Be Wesley

Several paintings must be mentioned that purport to be Wesley, but without any basis in provenance, in detail, or otherwise. There is so little consensus concerning Wesley's actual appearance that one wonders why there are not more false claimants.

The painting of a Charterhouse lad (a), presently hanging in John Street United Methodist Church in New York City, has no real claim to be the youth named John Wesley. The picture does show the nature of uniform that a schoolboy might have worn in that day. But it is not Wesley.

The Beinecke Library at Yale has a chalk drawing by John Downman (b) that has a tag on the back claiming that it is a portrayal of John Wesley. The image, however, bears no similarity to any known portrayal of the man and is very likely not of John Wesley, though it is probably eighteenth century.

Similar disclaimers could be made about the portrait of the gentleman whose painting was purchased by Frank Baker and is part of his collection in the Duke University library (c). Though it was said to be Wesley, there is no internal or external support for such a claim, even though the subject has long white hair, a long pointed nose, and is wearing Geneva bands. No one yet knows who it might be, and it remains so far unidentified.

At times, the portrait by A. L. Brandt of John Cennick (d), early Calvinist Methodist who wrote and published the poem on the "Wesley" teapot—"Be present at our table Lord, Be here and everywhere adored"—is said to be John Wesley.

The reputed Wesley portrait at Wesley House, Cambridge (e), shows an older man, which Wesley eventually became, but with long white hair, not typical of the older Wesley, and without bands or any other common feature of Wesley portraits. Some well-meaning person published a reproduction of the work as a product of Romney's brush, but without any rationale or provenance.[55]

Many other images vie for the honor of being considered as actual portraits or pictures of John Wesley. The same is true about many manuscripts and signatures that are claimed as authentic or possible Wesleyan artifacts that bear, in fact, no resemblance whatsoever to the handwriting of the man.

Among the candidate images is a bas-relief at Bridwell Library, Southern Methodist University, that has been honored as a representation of Wesley, as a typewritten note says on the back. It does, in fact, bear the three marks of a Wesley image: the locks at the bottom of long hair, a long pointed nose, and Geneva bands, the traditional garb of an eighteenth-century Anglican priest, as Wesley was. But nobody seems to have noticed the rosary in the person's right hand. There are a few people who claim that such a detail would not totally discount this image as being that of John Wesley. But there is nothing in its provenance that would even suggest such a fact. The rosary and the ornate (Baroque) frame instead indicate that the ivory carving is probably of a Roman Catholic priest, perhaps a member of a clerical order within the church.

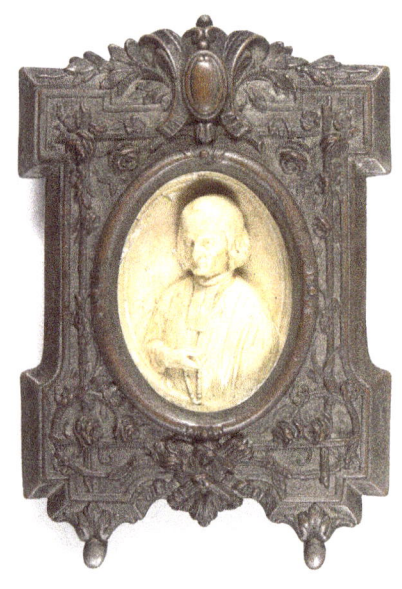

Other images in paintings or engravings turn up from time to time that are said to be early portraits of John Wesley, but

---

55. There is a publication by George Buckston Browne that argues that this portrait, sometimes attributed to George Romney, is actually the missing Joshua Reynolds portrait. *A Vindication of the Wesley-Romney Portrait at Wesley House, Cambridge* (London, 1926).

generally the claim is made more on the basis of personal inclination (often based on rumor, tradition, or the presence of the three typical features—long nose, curls on long hair, and Geneva tabs) than on actual evidence.

Before moving on, a word should be said about the so-called Reynolds portrait of Wesley—a work purportedly painted by Joshua Reynolds in 1755. Having had a portrait done by the generally acknowledged finest portrait painter of the time would certainly have enhanced Wesley's reputation, then and now.[56] Reynolds' sitting book refers to a "Mr. Westley" coming to have a portrait done in March 1755, a period for which there is no Wesley diary or journal.[57] There have been many conjectural Methodist identifications of the painting. One line of suggestion, however, asserts that the portrait hung for a time in Dangan Castle, County Meath, Ireland, until that structure was destroyed by fire. Dangan Castle was the home of Garrett Wesley, Baron of Mornington and later Viscount Wellesley. There is no way to know, therefore, whether the "Mr. Westley" mentioned in Reynolds's sitting book is our man or was part of the Irish family connection.[58] There is also no hint anywhere of the nature of the painting. Wesley himself does add to the mystery by commenting in 1789 that Romney was able to accomplish more in one hour than Sir Joshua Reynolds did in ten.[59] Whether this comment refers to his having actually sat for Reynolds or refers in general to Reynolds's reputation for slowness in creating a portrait is yet another matter for conjecture.

---

56. Certainly Reynolds was the most expensive portraitist, charging at times up to £150 for a portrait painting, whereas £30 was closer to the norm.

57. Kerslake goes into a very detailed explanation of the conjectures on this matter. 1:302. What he does not say is that there were several persons named John Wesley or John Westley at that time in London, some of them listed in the court cases and New Gate Prison records of the day.

58. Dangan was the family seat of the Earl of Mornington, Garrett Colley Wesley (1735–81), who was created Viscount Wellesley in 1760.

59. *Journal & Diaries*, January 5, 1789. It is hard to imagine Wesley sitting still for one hundred hours, since he actually spent over ten hours sitting for Romney.

Later Portraits of Wesley

As time went on after Wesley's death, many joined the parade of people publishing pictures of well-known figures like Wesley. Many entrepreneurs apparently had no compunction about making money by selling made-up engravings of the dead man. At times they simply copied previous engravings, often reversing them through incising a plate from a tracing of a previous printing, resulting in a reversed image when newly printed. Sometimes they combined features of previous paintings and engravings, such as the one that looks like a combination of a Williams-inspired background, a Zoffany-inspired pose, and a Barry-style face. But the subject, purportedly Wesley, is sometimes portrayed in a new way: for instance, the Hone image of Wesley preaching, but full length instead of three-fourths, and with tight long pants instead of a full robe. At times Wesley is later seen in a pose similar to Arnold, but he is portrayed as writing with the quill pen, which is not a feature found in the original Wesley portraits.

There is also a would-be copy of the Hamilton portrait of Wesley preaching with his palm vertical on the extended right hand and a pillow on the pulpit—but the portrait has a John Jackson style head. At some point after Jackson produced his semi-official portrait of Wesley, someone else felt that they could improve on Jackson by using Hamilton's pattern on the bottom half or perhaps improve Hamilton by putting Jackson's impression of Wesley on the top half (see p. 47 above).

Although beyond the regular scope of this study, the John Jackson portrait deserves notice because of its prevalence in the nineteenth century, the number of copies produced from it, and the nature of its origin. Faced with the lack of consensus among the contemporary portrayals of what Wesley looked like, the Book Room of the British Methodist Church wanted a "standard" portrait that could be used in their official publications, such as the frontispiece for the new hymnal they were producing in the 1820s. In the end, they chose John Jackson, R.A., to produce a portrait that supposedly synthesized the main features of the best portraits of Wesley during his lifetime. The unfortunate result probably does not portray his actual appearance at any point during his long life.

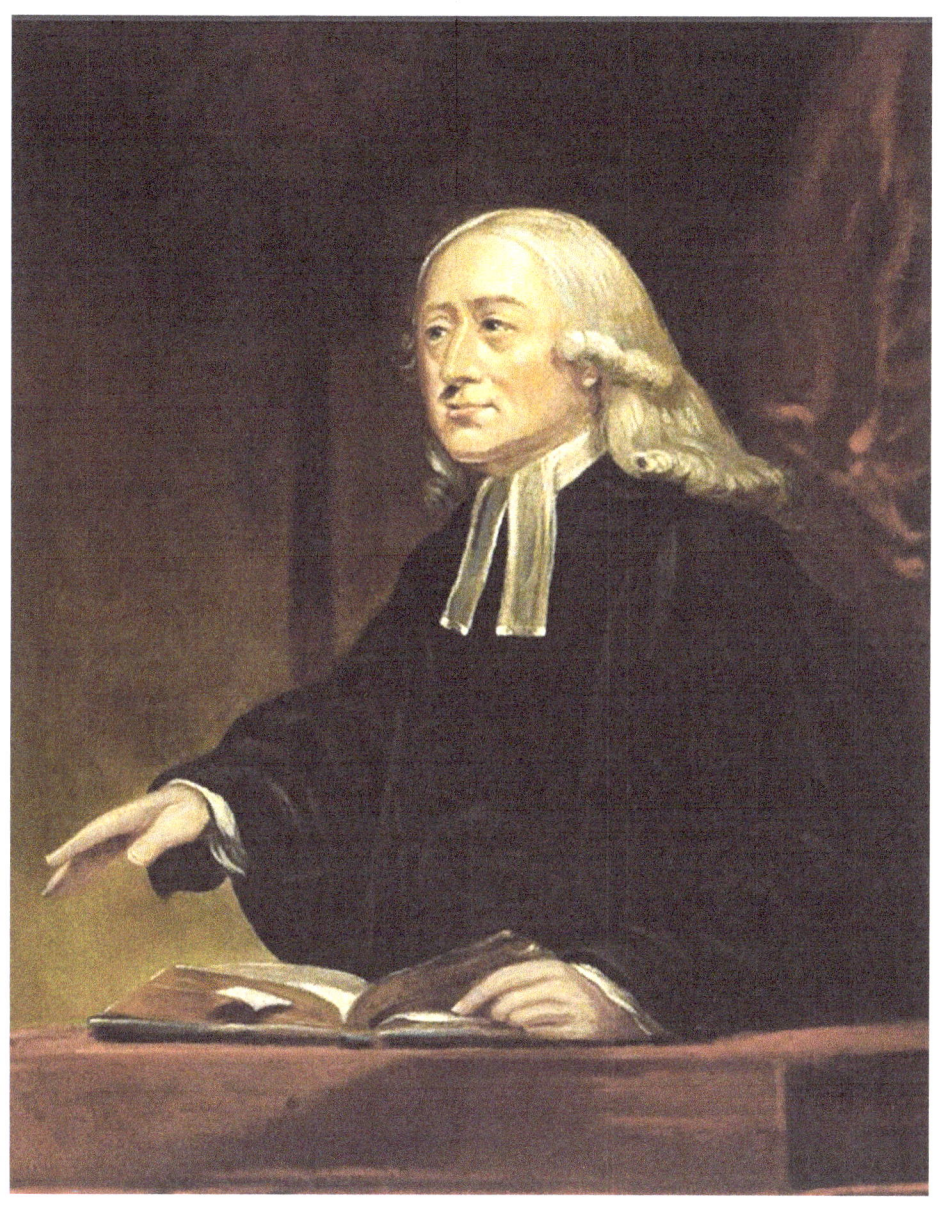

John Wesley, by John Jackson, R.A. (1827)

Nevertheless, the Jackson portrait slowly became the official "standard" in British Methodism, appearing as the frontispiece in the Wesleyan hymnal and many other publications, especially of the connectional book room. It also was the model for many copies, including the "Thursfield Smith" portrait, the "Castle" portrait, Nathaniel Currier's rendition, and many others.

There is perhaps no better example of how "standard" the Jackson portrait of Wesley became than the version of that pose reproduced in the "script" portrait of Wesley by Louis Glück (sometimes called Rosenthal), created during three years leading up to 1851.[60] This Jewish artist chose about twenty thousand words to replicate the typical or "standard" biography of Wesley, forming the fluid sentence lines into the recognizable shape of the "standard" portrait of Wesley by Jackson, finished three

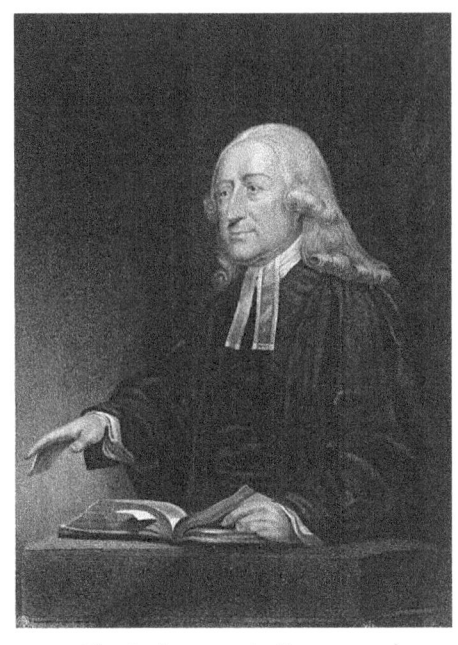

The Jackson portrait, engraved by T. A. Dean (1850)

decades earlier. The story starts in the lower left-hand corner with Wesley's birth and continues to wind around until it finishes in the same corner with the author's name.

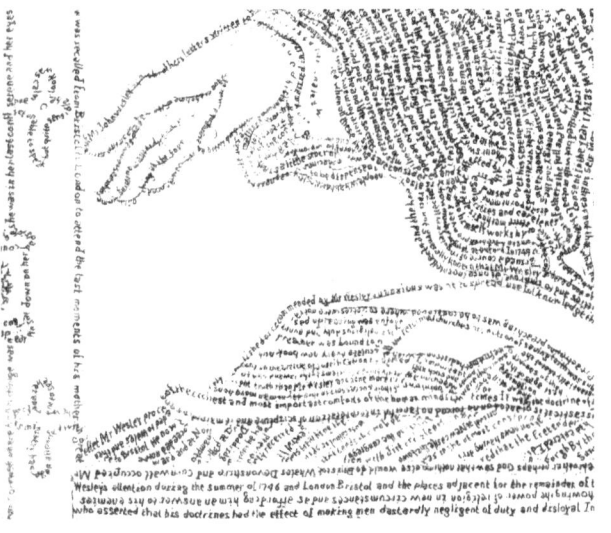

The Jackson portrait tried, unsuccessfully in most opinions, to synthesize the features of the contemporary attempts to capture Wesley's likeness. Although he does include the three main features common to most Wesley portraits—the long nose, the curls at the ends of his long hair, and the Geneva tabs—and uses the preaching pose common in the later portraits, Jackson fails to catch the facial shape and features that predominate in the "taken from life" portraits and busts that are acknowledged to be most faithful to his actual appearance.

60. WHS *Proceedings* 19 (Part 6, 1934): 129-32, and an article by Donald Ryan in 59 (Part 4, 2014): 136-48, both with illustrations. The second issue (c. 1857) is here reproduced.

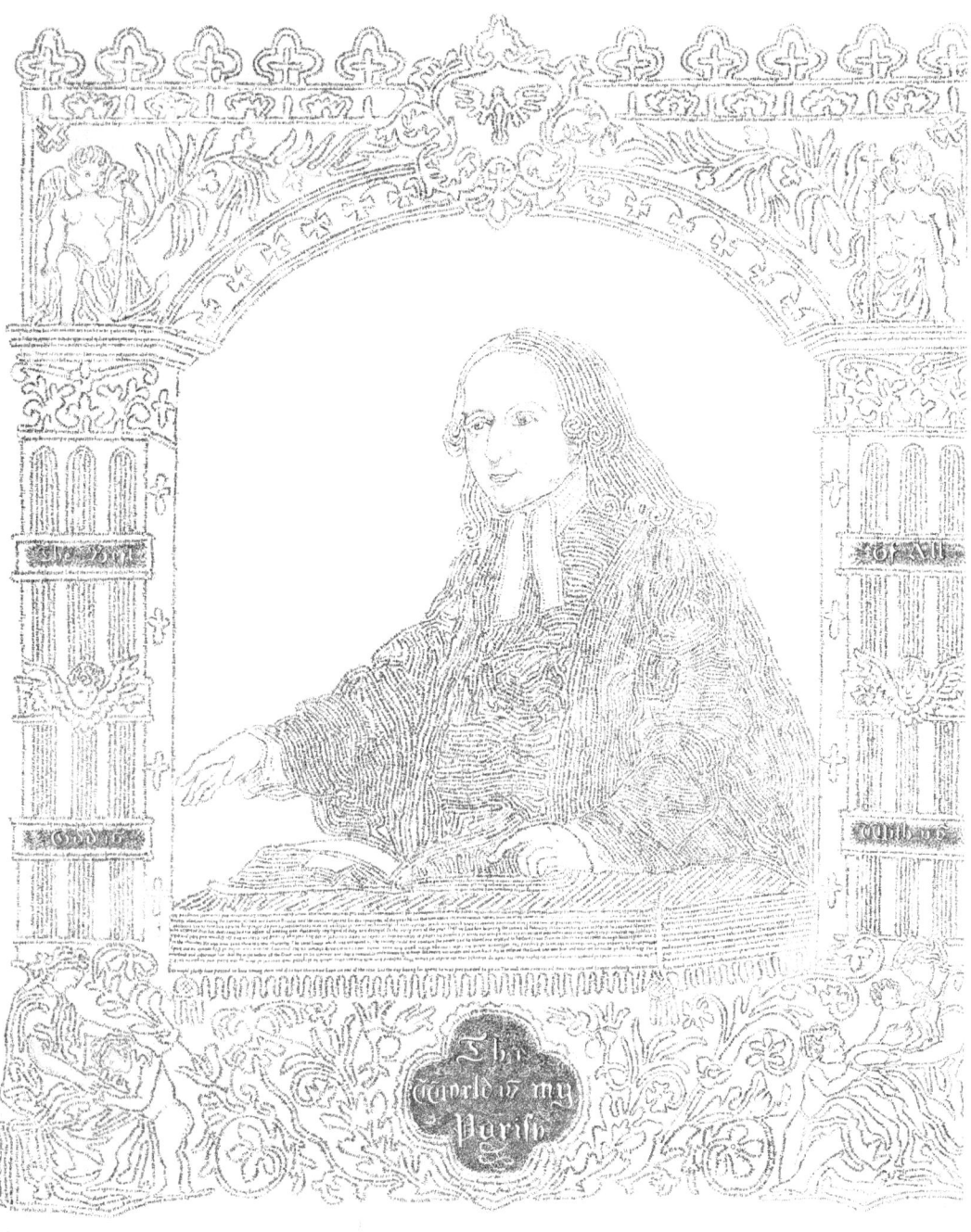

The "script" portrait, following Jackson, by Glück Rosenthal (1850s)

Portrait Painters

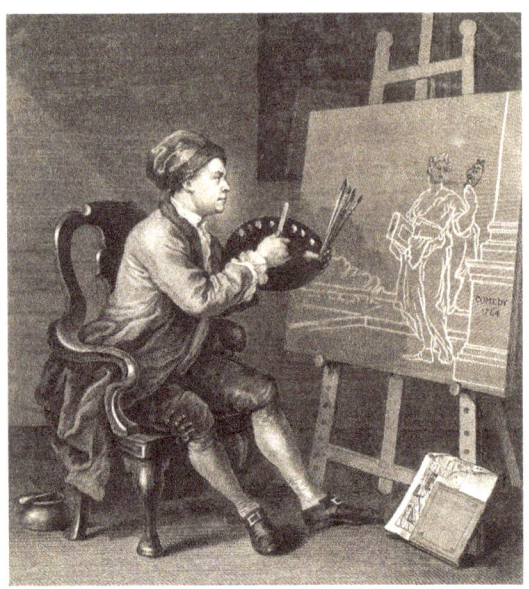

William Hogarth painting, *Self Portrait*

*T*he process by which these images, painted and printed, were produced by various artists—drawers, painters, and engravers— and then circulated in eighteenth-century England has some bearing on the story. There were of course no cameras, and the main issue at hand is not the question, "What did Wesley really look like?" Because of the great variety evident in the many images of the man, that question is virtually impossible to answer definitively in any case, even if you look carefully at every painted portrait and have a drawer full of contemporary engravings. The paintings and drawings that were produced by reputable artists, some even members of the Royal Academy who were looking directly at Wesley as the "sitter," are of primary interest for knowing just how Wesley appeared to people in the eighteenth century, but even these have widely different results.

Portrait paintings were often done by the artist in a studio, with the subject of the portrait present for as long as it took the painter to finish the face, hands, and any other details that demanded the presence of the sitter.[61] Sometimes the artist simply pulled the image out of his or her mind, as in the image of Hogarth painting the Muse. At other times, the artist made pencil drawings first, which could then serve three purposes: the drawing could be the preliminary stage of a subsequent

---

61. Stephen Lloyd and Kim Sloan, *The Intimate Portrait: Drawings, Miniatures, and Pastels from Ramsay to Lawrence* (Edinburgh: National Galleries of Scotland; London: The British Museum, 2008), 29.

painting, it could be the basis of an engraving or print, or it could be developed into a more finished state itself and become the final piece of art.

Either the artist or the sitter could initiate the production of a portrait. In the case of a famous personage, the artist could advance his own career by doing a painted portrait that developed some notoriety, either through the positive reaction of the person thus portrayed or through the reaction of the public, if the painting were exhibited and received popular acclaim, resulting in a demand for the proliferation of copies or prints.[62] The sittings

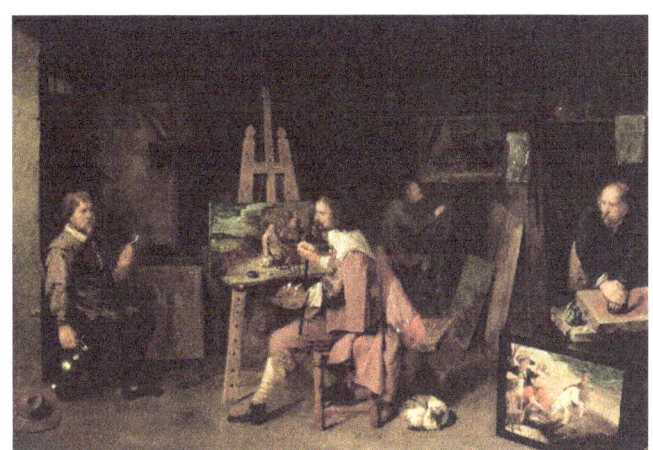
A painter's studio with helpers

entailed moderately lengthy periods of time in the artist's studio, anywhere from six to ten hours, usually on multiple occasions, and demanded a positive willingness on the part of the sitter to have his or her portrait painted. The time expended on such efforts and, if commissioned by the sitter, the charge for such a painting varied from artist to artist, but the range was usually between £6 and £25 (or 6 and 25 guineas), depending upon the size.[63] The cost in money could be borne by a patron, but the person being portrayed still had to pay the intangible cost of the sitting time, at least enough for the artist to finish the face and necessary details.

There were many instances when the artist/painter would produce a portrait that was a copy from another painting or print. Sometimes such copies were altered to fit the artist's prejudices or needs, sometimes becoming a caricature. Many times the portraits bore only minor changes, often visible in the details of the face. Occasionally the plates were simply re-engraved (especially if worn) or re-struck.

62. Ibid., 205.

63. Price was set in part by the size of the painting. Pointon, 44. A guinea was slightly more than a pound (£1 1s.) and was used to price books and expensive items.

Engravers, Printers, and Sellers

Relatively few people saw the original paintings that were produced in oils on canvas during that period. Even though paintings were often exhibited, especially by members of the Royal Academy, the entry fee (usually one shilling) was enough to keep out, as one newspaper wag in 1769 put it, "the noxious effluvia of the vulgar herd."[64] The portrayals, however, were often reproduced by woodcuts or engravings, usually by different artists than the painter, and were then circulated as prints that were much less expensive than the paintings. Sometimes such engravings were included as illustrations in publications that were widely available. Sometimes, engravers were also printers or sellers and had displays of their wares in their store windows, which became public art exhibitions for

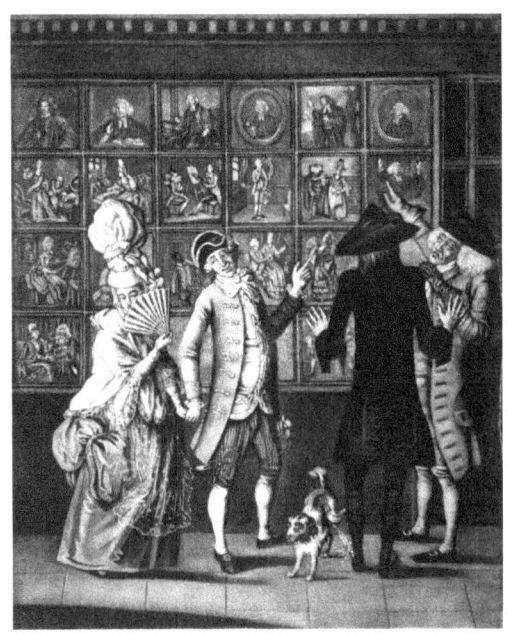

Bowles's storefront print exhibition.

people who could not even afford to buy the engravings.

Many of these secondary portrayals were copied from earlier etchings and woodcuts, sometimes with noticeable variations. In some cases, artists produced images of Wesley based on previous portrayals without any apparent direct contact with the man, but with the intent of caricaturing him. By the end of Wesley's long life, the inter-relationships among the various images of him becomes complex and in some cases quite confusing, due to the proliferation of anonymous artists producing these materials.

Generally, the original paintings or drawings were reproduced by one of three methods: woodcut, engraving (either line or mezzotint), or etching on metal. Lithography was

---

64. As mentioned (but uncited) by Helen Stewart in "The Royal Academy and the Hangmen," in *BBC Arts* (June 12, 2013).

not yet invented. Each involved very careful hand work: incising of wood for woodcuts, of metal for engraved plates, or of a wax or varnish "ground" to allow an acid wash to etch a metal plate. These methods were, at the time, the primary means of printing reproductions of the paintings.

For woodcuts, the artist usually cut away the wood for those areas of the print that would be left white, creating the raised surfaces of the wood that would carry the ink to the paper. Woodcuts were, however, becoming less prevalent in the eighteenth century, since engravers began more often to use incised metal plates (usually made of copper), which were more hardy and could be cut more finely. The method could be either relief printing, as with most woodcuts, or intaglio printing, where the ink was transferred from a groove in the plate rather than the surface.

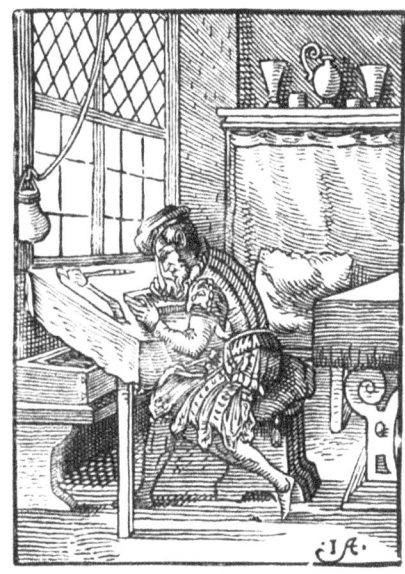

A medieval woodcarver at work.

The groove of an engraving was carved into the plate by means of graver or "burin," a steel tool like an awl, which came in a variety of shapes and sizes. The artist could also scratch fine parts of the design into the plate by means of a sharp dry-point tool. In either case, this method allowed ink to be transferred to the paper by the intaglio method—that is, after being inked, the surface of the plate was wiped clean, leaving ink only in the grooves. The ink was then transferred to the paper from the groove rather than having the ink on a raised surface, like type or a woodcut. Mezzotint involved the use of some other tools, such as rockers and burnishers, which could roughen the plates and sometimes left burrs that held more ink. This method could give the print more texture and finer gradation of tones than line engravings or woodcuts.

For etching, the ground, made of wax or other covering layer on the surface of the metal, was incised by means of sharp etching needles or other tools that exposed the metal underneath, which then could be etched by an acid wash into which the plate was dipped. Wherever the ground had been cut away, the metal was exposed to the acid, which then would bite into the metal—the timing of this exposure would determine the depth of the bite across the plate and therefore the amount (thickness or darkness) of the ink that would be printed.

At times, engraved portrayals were revised, either because the plate had become worn through use and needed to be revitalized or because the artist wanted to change part of the image. This process involved making part of the copperplate smooth by hammering on the back side, then re-incising the front, trying to make the new lines and the old lines at the edge of the revised portion (usually the face) continue as flawlessly as possible. Figuring out the sequence of these "states" of the revised engravings can involve a tedious process of close examination of the prints and a careful consideration of related evidence, since the plate is rarely extant.

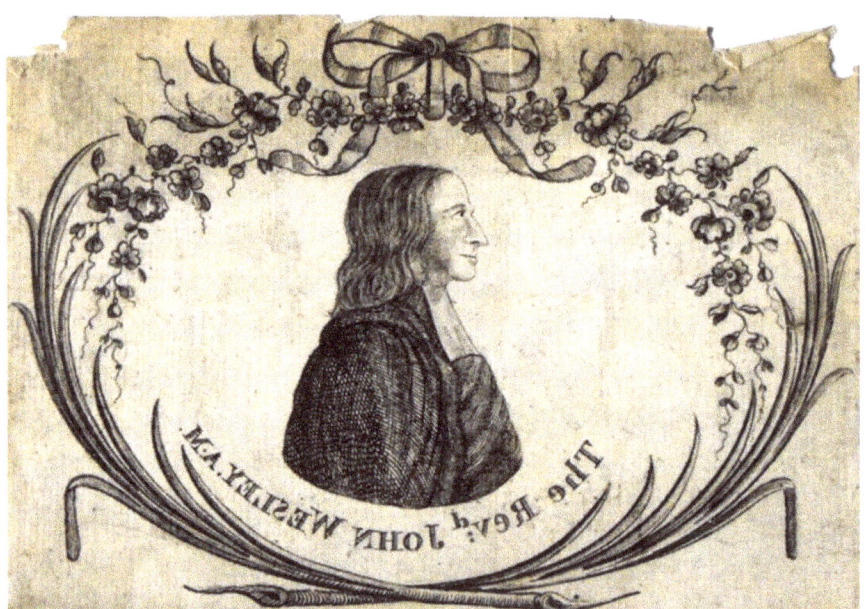

Tracing paper image (usually in reversed form) used to make engraving copperplate.

Often the engraver copying a previous work produced an image that was flipped or reversed, such as the Greenwood copy of the Hone painting or engraving. This method involved tracing the picture on tissue paper, often held in place over the image by means of four pins in the corners. The resulting picture was then copied onto the copperplate in the same direction, resulting in a reversed image when printed.[65] The best example of this process is the tracing image that is properly reversed on paper, which will result in a correct version of the lettering and picture when cut into the printing plate backwards (see opposite page).[66]

Many of the engravers mentioned above are nearly anonymous individuals now, when it comes to our knowing anything about them beyond their artistic production. They were not allowed as members of the Royal Academy until late in the century.

Some of the engravers contracted with artists to produce

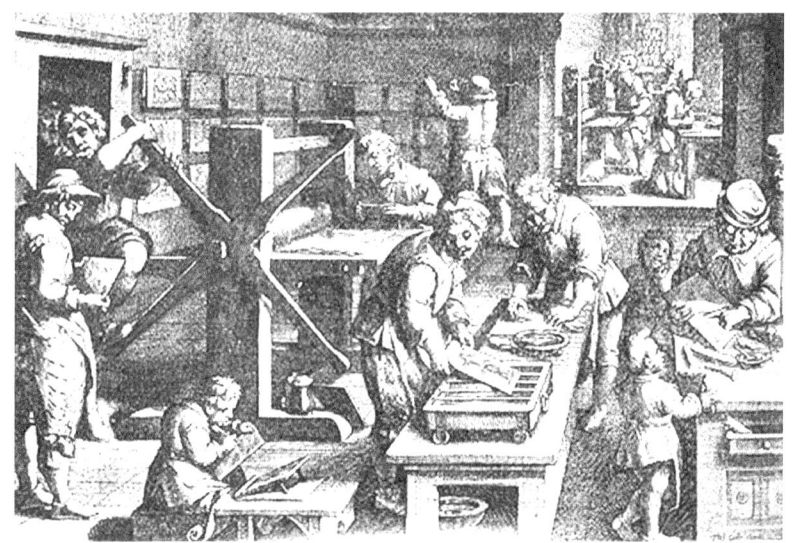

Print tools such as this sixteenth-century copperplate press did not change much over the years.

copies of their work. Many of the British artists and engravers lived in the London area, clustering around the centers of culture and printing in Fleet Street, Westminster, or Cornhill. Sometimes the engravers were also printers and/or sellers, and their shops were multi-purpose establishments. When one died or went out of business, their collection of plates was often sold to another engraver, who usually burnished off the previous engraver's name and added his own, producing another "state" or refurbishing of the print.

---

65.   See above, p. 28 for Greenwood and p. 25 for Ranmoor.

66.   Seen on "Recent Acquisitions, July 2013" list, item 18, John Price, Antiquarian Books, London, Eng.

This process accounts for some of the similarities among the various reproductions, especially by such persons as Robert Sayer, Carington Bowles (1724–93), and others. Carington Bowles had likely purchased or shared the plates of Sayer, a common arrangement.[67] Sayer had already accumulated plates from many engravers, such as Henry Overton the Younger. Overton was in business at the White Horse, without Newgate, until 1764 or so, when Sayer took over the business and moved to Fleet Street. Sayer also seems to have taken over James Faber's plates in the purchase of Overton's business.

Henry Parker's business is usually associated with Cornhill, Robert Sayer's with Fleet Street, and Carington Bowles's with St. Paul's Church Yard. But they worked together on many projects.

Nathaniel Hone is acknowledged as the painter in each of these inscriptions pictured below for mezzotints of his painting. The first is at the bottom of the engraving by John Greenwood (Hone's painting reversed) printed in December 1770 for Robert Sayer, who was working with John and Carington Bowles (the son) by the 1760s. The second is found on an engraving of the Hone portrait that was a copy of the original and also published in December 1770. It was printed for Carington Bowles, who is also cited as *excudit*—"he engraved it." And the third inscription comes from a copy of the Hone printed for Carington Bowles II and Samuel Carver, who joined forces in the 1790s at 69 St. Paul's Church Yard.

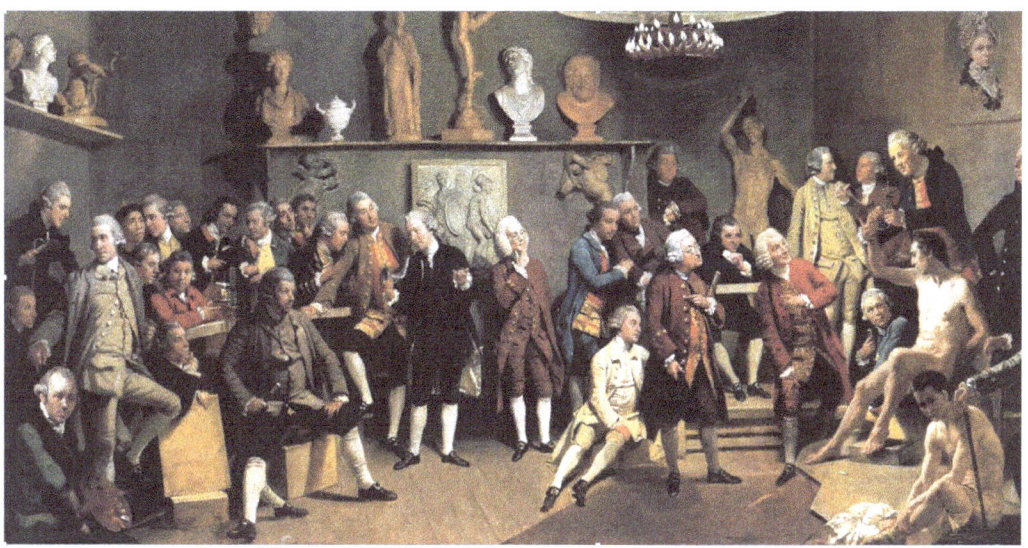

Portrait of the Academicians of the Royal Academy (1771–72), by Johann Zoffany.

Study of Wesley Portraits

*T*he fact that there have been no serious studies of the Wesley portraits that are contemporaneous with his life is somewhat amazing. Nearly every survey of the man's life mentions that the portraits exhibit a wild variation, save for those three common details—nose, curls, tabs. And there has been some general work done on enumerating the Wesley portraits, notably in the early pages of the Wesley Historical Society *Proceedings* at the turn of the last century.

But very few people mention that even notable painters—members of the Royal Academy, who were carefully monitored for their talent and seemed to have reached the pinnacle of their craft—were not able to portray a common visage to which one could point as a reliable image of Wesley's actual appearance. Most of the comments, especially from early Wesley scholars, suffer from the same Methodist triumphalism and irrational bias and lack even the beginnings of careful analysis that mark such literary works as Luke Tyerman's biography of Wesley.

Even Wesley himself is of little help when it comes to identifying the best image of his face. The portraits that he comments upon in a favorable light, using such phrases as "an exact likeness," "a most striking likeness," "the best that ever was taken," are of little or no help in coming to a reasonable conclusion as to his actual appearance. His favorite portraits, like the later ones (after he was sixty years old) by Hunter, Hamilton, Romney, and Arnold—all reputable artists of the day—are not

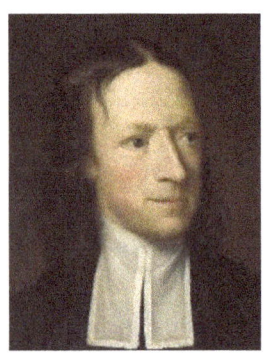 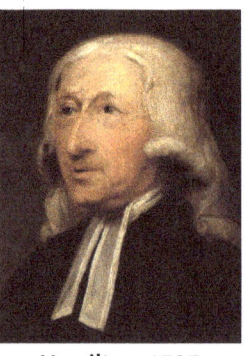 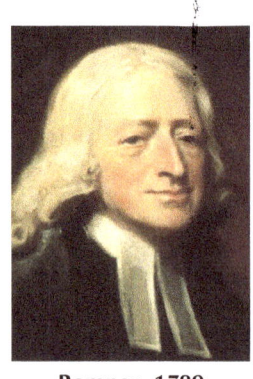 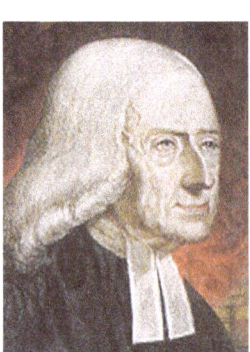

| Hunter, 1765 | Hamilton, 1787 | Romney, 1789 | Arnold, 1790 |

even similar in their appearance. The ones that Wesley chose for the *Arminian Magazine* in the 1770s and 1780s (p. 39 above) are as variant as any group that one could pick.

The engravings that were not directly taken from the paintings show an even greater divergence from any norm that might be drawn from the paintings. The reproductions in Telford's *Sayings and Portraits* are not good and often not identified carefully (see above, pp. 2–3), but the engravings produced by craftsmen and craftswomen during that day are apparently no closer to reality. A selection from that category also demonstrates amazing degrees of variation. The artisans are more interested in sales than in accuracy. No artist claims universally acknowledged exactness or credits the art piece with any sort of faithfulness to visual reality. The purpose of their business is to make money and, crass as it may seem, that is the thing about which many of them are most concerned.

Granted, there is some difference in time, in artists' talents, in limits of the medium (a fine painting is much more capable of portraying details than a rough woodcut), and in the time allowed for creating an image. But the interests of the painter or engraver in getting beyond what they see, as if they were cameras, in order to portray the artist's independent view of the person's character, influence, or demeanor (or perhaps what he thought the public might believe in those terms to lead them to buy the picture), seems perhaps even more to interfere with their capability to produce an accurate portrayal of how Wesley actually looked.

Beginning in the last half of the twentieth century, Wesley studies finally began to exhibit the critical temper that had marked historical work in general for over a century. John Kerslake in 1977 included John Wesley in his fine study of *Early Georgian Portraits,* focusing on the National Portrait Gallery, London, but made the comment, "A detailed critical survey of the [Wesley] portraiture is overdue."[68] He pointed out, for instance, that a careful study of the bust of Wesley attributed to Roubiliac showed that it was neither by that artist nor by Silvester, a hypothesis presented in

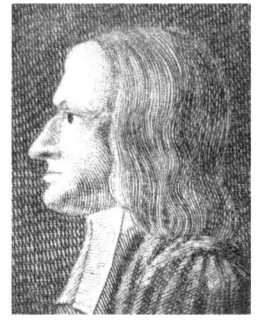 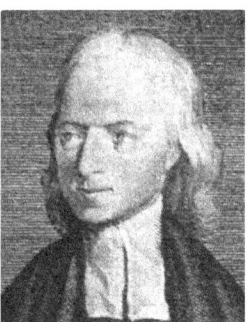 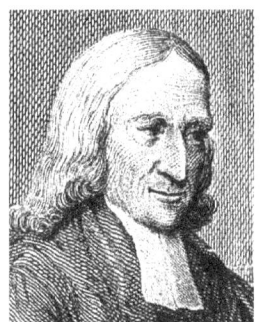 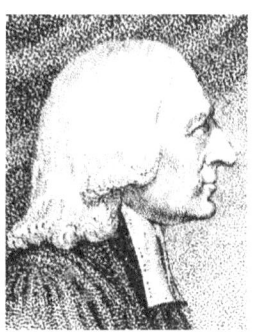

| After Bone, 1782 | Ranmoor, 1785 | Tookey, 1791 | Miller, 1790 |

1928. The stories surrounding the so-called Reynolds portrait of Wesley have also resulted in the frequent debunking of the idea that Joshua Reynolds ever created a painting of John Wesley the Methodist. Many such stories, associating portraits of Wesley with famous painters, are as fictional as many of the literary "twice-told tales" that abound, claims that have become accepted as factual simply because of their long existence and repetition but have no basis in historical fact.

Marcia Pointon's *Hanging the Head* (1993) may be the best recent general study of British portraiture, but there is yet a near vacuum of careful studies of the Wesley portraits. Even the most recent study, a 215-page publication by Samuel Rogal,

---

68. Kerslake, 1:301.

is rife with outright errors, illustrated by horribly unhelpful reproductions, and filled with untested opinions carried over from Telford's old study, *Sayings and Portraits of John Wesley*, produced in 1924. Very little careful analytical work has been done on the Wesley portraits, save for the recent articles by Peter Forsaith, currently the Research Fellow at the Oxford Centre for Methodism and Church History at Oxford Brookes University.[69]

The fact that very little study has been directed toward the Wesley portraits is understandable, given the dearth of likeness among the extant contemporary portrayals of the man. The desire for a "standard" portrait as early as 1824 tells us that the various earlier attempts to display his likeness had failed, just as the synthetic approach of John Jackson would fail in the early nineteenth century.

What some people do not realize, however, is that the twentieth-century portraits are no closer to helping us know how the man actually appeared. These attempts have generally been ignored by anyone seriously interested in discovering his actual image. The focus has changed to his thought and actions. Much has been written in the last two centuries that tries to capture the theological bent of Wesley's mind and the direction, if not the details, of his many activities. Such a task is not easy.[70] One must take into account the changes resulting from his development, his controversial nature, his growing legend even during his lifetime, and the changing context.

The same is true with his physical appearance. He lived a long life—over eighty-seven years. The wear and tear of many years would have taken its toll on the man. And yet he is still portrayed by some scholars and artists as having one mind throughout and as having one visage over an extended lifetime. There were obviously no cameras available, no photographs taken. And the hand-done paintings, drawings, and engravings say as much about each artist's larger conception of the person as they do about the person the artists have tried to portray.

At this point in time, neither the visual nor the intellectual image of the man can be recaptured in full. But the attempt is a worthwhile exercise, even if only partially possible.

---

69. Articles on the Russell portraits of Charles and Samuel Wesley, the Romney portraits of John; and Methodist iconography in general.

70. *The Elusive Mr. Wesley*, 2nd ed. (Nashville: Abingdon, 2005).

Concluding Comments

$\mathcal{L}$et us finally end this brief survey by gathering together the major portraits done of Wesley during his lifetime and commenting on them as groups. One can see why, at the beginning, it is important to realize that one cannot criticize these works based on either their artistic merit or their proximity to portraying the man accurately, as he actually looked. Although persons may have individual opinions about artistic merit, no one will never know the latter—what Wesley's actual visage was.

Among these portraits there is a significant developmental trend. There are generally three types of depiction that can be used to differentiate the major groupings: (1) in a more *scholarly* pose, with many books present, including a prominent Bible; (2) in a *preaching* mode, holding a Bible, with the other hand raised; and (3) in a more neutral pose, typically associated with notable or *famous* people, focusing simply on the face. In that light, one should also note that the earlier and latest portraits tend to be of the academic sort, including those by Williams, Zoffany, and Arnold. The preaching type of portrayal tends to predominate in the period from 1766 to 1788, including those by Hone, Russell, and Hamilton. What have been called the more neutral portraits are interspersed among the others: those by such artists as Hunter, Romney, and Horsley. These types then represent somewhat competing images of the man—competing for iconic prominence during his lifetime—and can be seen as ways of emphasizing different sides of an elusive figure who is both a learned theologian/teacher and a caring pastor/preacher.

Aside from the cartoons or critical sketches, which often portray a ranting preacher, such as those by Hogarth, the paintings and etchings that portray Wesley preaching show him to be very calm. Except for the Hamilton painting, in which the mouth is slightly open, Wesley is always portrayed with a closed mouth, not unusual for a portrait but perhaps somewhat unnatural, given the man's propensity for talking with friends or strangers and preaching frequently to small and large congregations of people. Given the variety of portrayals and the differing quality of the images, Adam Clarke seems to be correct when he says

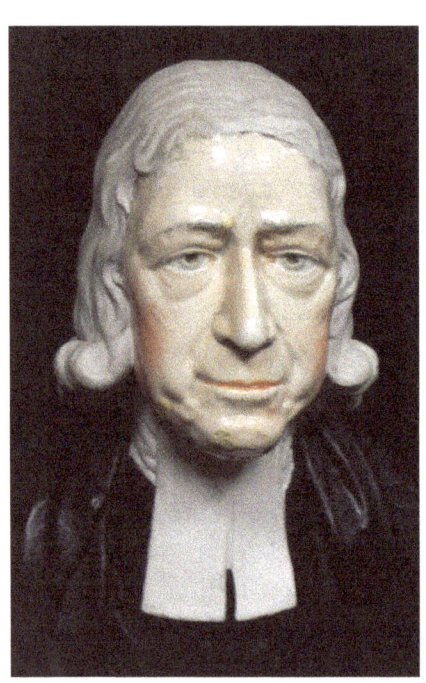

that the Enoch Wood bust is the closest portrayal of his actual visage. No matter how one views the application of these different sorts of images, one can say, however, with some certainty which portraits Wesley himself liked, or perhaps which reproductions of the portraits he liked. He may have seen the portraits themselves, but most people would not have had the opportunity.

But there is little consensus on self-conception, however, to be derived from looking at these four favorites: the Downes engraving of the Williams portrait, used by Wesley as the frontispiece for the *Explanatory Notes Upon the New Testament* (1755); the Bland engraving of the Hone portrait, used as the frontispiece for the *Explanatory Notes Upon the Old Testament* (1766); the Hamilton portrait, which he commented positively upon; and the Spilsbury engraving of the Romney portrait, which he apparently gave as a gift to some of his friends. One of these favorites shows him as a scholar, probably teaching; one of them is a sober bust-style portrait; and the other two show him preaching, outdoors under a tree and inside at a pulpit. In every case, however, he does appear to be the respectable Oxford graduate, dressed in his clergy garb, never ranting, much less frothing at the mouth—in fact, his mouth is almost always closed. He is the picture of saintly academic refinement. This image seems to continue beyond Wesley's death in the public mind with the prominence of the Arnold/Barry seated scholar image and the Edridge profile of a calm preaching Wesley.

But one must include in this list of favorites the portrayal that he himself chose as the first frontispiece for his monthly publication, the *Arminian Magazine* (1778). The viewer is left smiling, if not laughing, and asking, Why? Why would Wesley choose such a picture? Did he really think he looked like that? Did he guess or hope that people thought he looked like that? Perhaps, as Pointon says, the quality of the artwork is not at issue here. Perhaps the actual visage of the person is not the point one should be raising. But rather, what does this portrait say about the artist or about the person being portrayed? Perhaps one should be wondering also about their view of the public at that time, or perhaps the public's view of them?

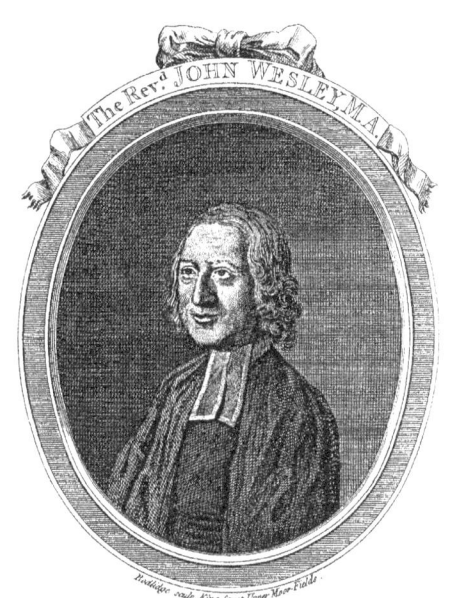

Even though one is inclined to say that this first *Arminian Magazine* portrait is, next to the Ranmoor portrait showing him with no shoulders whatsoever, perhaps a portrayal of the meekest, mildest, mousiest, or should one say the most pious-looking person in England at the time, it is difficult to think that Wesley would have chosen this portrait to convey to his people and others the essence of the Methodist leader who had faced rioters in the fields, who considered himself a powerful preacher and strong leader, and who was trying to lead the battle against the Calvinists in Britain. Perhaps piety and meekness is what Wesley was hoping to portray in his use of that picture. If so, it was one of the few times that he completely failed to calculate accurately the public response, and one of the few times that he really did not understand the basic elements of this non-verbal but very powerful means of communication with the people called Methodists as well as the wider British public.

Likewise, it is difficult to imagine that the artists, while trying to sell their wares in order to make a living, would stray far from the actual visage of a man who could frequently be seen around London and, in fact, throughout the British Isles. Something, however, inspired them to portray Wesley in many ways that defy present-day imagination. It is one thing to be ignorant of the actual appearance of someone like Jesus Christ, who lived over two millennia ago. But to have difficulty coming up with a commonly acknowledged portrait of Wesley's image from less than three centuries ago, when there are so many visual and literary descriptions of the man in existence, is somewhat mind-boggling.

People today must recognize, however, that these portraits still carry the weight of being one of the best sources of contemporary historical information for our own understanding of Wesley in his own day. Perhaps one needs to remember Carradine's advice to her boss, Inspector Grant, in Josephine Tey's novel: "The real history is written in forms not meant as history."

Acknowledgments

$\mathcal{T}$his work is the result of nearly sixty years of interest in the graphic representations of John Wesley. My introduction to the topic came from my mentor, Frank Baker, who kept cardboard boxes containing engravings of Wesley and others under his ping-pong table at home. The interest became more serious as the disparity among the various portraits became incorporated into the visual material used to illustrate my Methodism classes. In the 1980s the varied portraits became a sign of the larger problem that one has in trying to characterize the thinking of a person who lived a long a productive life over two centuries earlier.

The tercentenary of Wesley's birth, 2003, provided many opportunities to present this issue. The American Academy of Religion annual meeting in Atlanta, GA, the American Methodist Historical Society meeting at Drew University, and the tercentenary celebration at Duke University became vehicles for spreading this concern. The PowerPoint reproductions of the various paintings, busts, and engravings of Wesley done during his lifetime became a tool for analyzing and interpreting the life and teachings of Wesley. The immediate predecessor of this book was the 2011 international video-cast of my Wesley Lecture at the Nazarene Theological Seminary in Manchester, England, at the invitation of Geordan Hammond, Director of the Manchester Wesley Research Centre there. The work was intended for reproduction in the *Wesley and Methodist Studies* produced by the Centre, but the length and complexity of the work exceeded their normal limits.

This work is part of a larger effort to bring together an illustrated catalog of Wesley portraits, especially those executed during his lifetime or shortly thereafter. Librarians, archivists, collectors, and students around the globe have helped tremendously in this effort.

Particular thanks is due to Brian Milford, Chief Executive of Abingdon Press, for encouraging and accepting this work for publication. In the midst of a terribly busy move to new quarters, the staff there has been unstintingly helpful. David Teel, Laura Wheeler, Katie Johnston, and Paul Franklyn have been particularly helpful.

This work focuses on the illustrations, many of which are in the public domain and are readily available. Some are more scarce and some are in the hands of collectors and institutions that are listed in the section below. Special permission was required by several of them, which is also listed specifically. The main depositories that were used include the Frank Baker Collection at Duke University; the collections at the Huntingdon Library of Pasadena, CA; the National Portrait Gallery and the British Museum in London; the Luke Tyerman Collection at Drew University; the Special Collections at Bridwell Library of Southern Methodist University; and the Methodist Archives at the Rylands University Library of Manchester. Many friends and experts in Wesley Studies have helped over the years, especially my wife, Karen Heitzenrater; my colleagues Peter Forsaith, Geordan Hammond, and Randy Maddox; and my deceased mentors, Frederick Maser, Albert Outler, and Frank Baker. *Deo gratias.*

List of Illustrations and Permissions

Where a painting has a particular home, permission has been granted and credit has been given to one of those fourteen places. Most of the illustrations are of engravings that are in the public domain and are in my own personal collection or in the Frank Baker Collection of the David L. Rubenstein Library, Duke University, as well as other depositories that have been examined such as the Bridwell Library, Southern Methodist University; the Archives and History Collection, Drew University; the Huntingdon Library, Pasadena. CA; the Woodruff Library, Emory University; the Methodist Archives, Rylands University Library of Manchester; the World Methodist Museum, Lake Junaluska; and the Oxford Centre for Wesley and Methodism at Oxford Brookes University, England.

The title of an engraving is given unless it simply gives the name. The date of artist, painting, and publishing is given when known. The notation (a), (b), and so forth, indicates presence of illustrations left to right on page or top to bottom.

ii   "John Wesley, M.A., Fellow of Lincoln Colledge," painted by John Harley (H&S, after John Williams); c. 1745; photo by the author at Wesley College, Bristol, England; presently at the Old Rectory, Epworth, England. Reproduced by kind permission of the Trustees of Epworth Old Rectory, © TMCP 2016.

1   Line engraving, anonymous (possibly by John Downes, d. 1774); published Oct. 7, 1741.

2   Engravings published in John Telford, *Sayings and Portraits of John Wesley* (London: Epworth Press, 1924), 211, 91, 127.

      (a) Engraving by William Greatbach (fl. 1849–60); published in 1851, from a drawing attributed to Thomas Worlidge (1700–66).

(b) Engraved by James Watson (c. 1739–90); 1765, from a painting by Robert Hunter (fl. 1750–80).

(c) Engraved by Jonathan Spilsbury (c. 1737–1812); 1789, from a painting by George Romney (1734–1802).

3   Engravings published in John Telford, *Sayings and Portraits,* 123, 175, 107.

(a) Engraved by James Fittler, A.R.A. (1758–1835); 1788, from a painting by William Hamilton, R.A. (1751–1801).

(b) Engraved by N. Nasmyth; 1791.

(c) Engraved by Bodlidge for *Arminian Magazine;* 1778.

4   (a) George Romney (1734–1892); self portrait, n.d.

(b) Williams Hamilton, R.A., painted by Thomas Lawrence, R.A. (1769–1830); 1788.

(c) George Vertue (1684–1756), painted by Jonathan Richardson; 1733.

(d) Johann Zoffany, R.A. (1733–1810); self portrait, c. 1766.

5   (a) Enoch Wood, painted by Henry Room, 1827.

(b) John Flaxman, R.A, (1755–1826), painted by Henry Howard; c. 1797.

(c) Nathaniel Hone, R.A. (1718–84); self portrait, c. 1760.

(d) Joshua Reynolds, R.A. (1723–92); self portrait, c. 1766.

6   "John Wesley, M.A., Fellow of Lincoln College, Oxford." engraved by George Vertue (1684–1756); 1742, proof of state 1. Frank Baker Collection of Wesleyana and British Methodism, David M. Rubenstein Rare Book & Manuscript Library, Duke University.

9   "John Wesley, M.A." Engraved by John Downes? (d. 1774), published Oct. 7, 1741.

11   "John Wesley," painted by John Michael Williams (1710–c. 1780), 1742–43. Frontispiece, W. J. Townsend, et al., *A New History of Methodism* (London: Hodder and Stoughton, 1909).

12   (a) "John Wesley, M.A; Fellow of Lincoln College, Oxford," engraved by George Vertue (after Williams); 1745, proof of state 2. Baker Collection, Rubenstein Library, Duke University.

(b) "John Wesley, M.A; Fellow of Lincoln College, Oxford," engraved by George Vertue; 1745, state 3. Baker Collection, Rubenstein Library, Duke University.

13   "John Wesley, M.A; Fellow of Lincoln College, Oxford," engraved by

Thomas Bakewell (fl. 1743–1749), "Moravian Portrait"; published c. 1745–49; after Vertue state 3 reversed, with sister Emilia's poem on scroll.

14   (a) Mezzotint by James Faber, Jr. (1684–1756); published Sept. 10, 1743 (after Williams).

        (b) Engraved by Carington Bowles (fl.1752–93); 1770 (after Williams).

        (c) Engraved by James Watson; 1765 (after Williams).

        (d) Engraved by Richard Houston (c. 1721–75); 1780 (after Williams).

15   Painted by John Harley, "Mission House" 3/4 length portrait; c. 1745 (after Williams). Courtesy of the Oxford Centre for Methodism and Church History, Oxford Brookes University, Oxford, England.

16   Painted by John Harley (H&S, after John Williams); c. 1745. Photo by author at Wesley College, Bristol; presently at the Old Rectory, Epworth, England. Reproduced by kind permission of the Trustees of Epworth Old Rectory, © TMCP 2016.

17   (a) Mezzotint by John Tinney (1706–61); c. 1760.

        (b) Mezzotint by Johann Jakob Haid (1704–67); c. 1765.

18   Engraved by John Downes, frontispiece to *Explanatory Notes Upon the New Testament*, 1755.

20   "Religion, Superstition, and Fanaticism." Painted and engraved by William Hogarth (1697–1764); 1762.

21   (a) Anonymous engraver, "Perfection" (Devil's head); 1778.

        (b) James Green, Wesley as a teaching fox; 1779.

22   Painted by Robert Hunter (fl. 1750–80); 1765. Reproduced with permission of the Trustees of Wesley's Chapel, City Road.

24   Mezzotint by James Watson (c. 1739–90), 1765.

25   (a) Anonymous copyist, after Hunter; n.d.

        (b) Anonymous engraving of Ranmoor portrait;1785.

27   Painted by Nathaniel Hone, R.A. (1718–84); 1766 © National Portrait Gallery, London.

28   Mezzotint engraved by John Greenwood (1727–92); 1770.

29   "Cole" portrait, painted by anonymous copyist; n.d. (c. 1771). Courtesy, the Drew University Library Methodist Collection.

30   Detail of "Cole" portrait, reversed.

31   (a) Detail of Hone painting.

(b) Detail of engraving by Bland, frontispiece for "Explanatory Notes Upon the Old Testament, 1766."

(c) Detail of Greenwood mezzotint, reversed.

32   Bland engraving of painting by John Russell, R.A. (1745–1806); 1773. Baker Collection, Rubenstein Library, Duke University.

34   (a) Mezzotint by John Gainer (fl. 1772–79); 1775.

(b) Detail of portrait by John Russell; 1773 (original, now lost.) Reproduced with permission of the Trustees of Wesley's Chapel, City Road.

35   Anonymous engraving of "Miss Dalrymple" and "The Pious Preacher"; 1775.

36   (a) William Greatbach (fl. 1849–60), engraving of Thomas Worlidge drawing of Wesley preaching (from life in 1760s?); frontispiece for Isaac Taylor, *Wesley and Methodism*, 1851.

(b) Engraving by John Lodge (fl. 1754–94), *Sunday Magazine;* March 4, 1781.

37   Anonymous frontispiece to *Fanatical Conversion;* 1778.

39   (a) Engraved by Bodlidge, *Arminian Magazine*; 1778.

(b) Anonymous engraver, *Arminian Magazine;* 1779.

(c) Anonymous engraver, *Arminian Magazine;* 1783.

40   Bust by Enoch Wood (1759–1840); c. 1782, photo by the author.

42   John Flaxman, Wedgewood designer; c. 1780s.

(a) Flaxman drawing for Wedgewood ceramic; n.d.

(b) White Wedgewood parian on black.

(c) White on green Wedgewood cameo of Wesley.

(d) Anonymous sculptor, Samuel Manning (?) bust of Wesley (also incorrectly called for a time the "Roubiliac" bust), © National Portrait Gallery, London.

43   (a) Engraved by J. Palin, after Edridge.

(b) Miniature, painted by Henry Bone, R.A. (1755–1834), 1780.

(c) Engraved by R. Page (fl. 1813–23), after Edridge.

(d) Anonymous profile engraving, after Bone, 1782.

45   Painted by William Hamilton, R.A. (1751–1801); 1787. © National Portrait Gallery, London.

46   Engraved by James Fittler, A.R.A. (1758–1835); 1788.

47   (a) Engraved by Richard Roffe (fl. 1797–1828); 1799.

        (b) Anonymous engraver; 1791.

        (c) Anonymous engraver; after 1827.

48   Painted by George Romney (1734–1802; 1789. © Philadelphia Museum of Art).

50   Mezzotint by Jonathan Spilsbury (c. 1737–1812); 1789. Baker Collection, Rubenstein Library, Duke University.

51   (a) Anonymous engraving (colored in) of Romney.

        (b) Anonymous engraving of Romney "fur" portrait.

        (c) Miniature, painted by William Grimaldi (1751–1830); after Romney.

        (d) Copy of Romney, perhaps by the artist; n.d. © National Portrait Gallery, London.

52   Painted by Thomas Horsley (fl. 1780–1790); c. 1790, state 3. Courtesy of Sunderland Museum & Winter Gardens.

54   Johann Zoffany/Sylvester Harding painting; n.d.

55   Engravings taken from Zoffany/Harding:

        (a) Engraved by Francesco Bartolozzi, R.A. (1757–1815); n.d.

        (b) Engraved by S. Gardiner; n.d.

        (c) Engraved by William Nelson Gardiner (1766–1814); n.d.

        (d) Detail from Zoffany/Harding painting.

56   Miniature oil painting by R. Arnold (fl. 1770–1810); 1790.

58   Copies of Arnold:

        (a) Engraved by William Ridley (1764–1838); after 1809.

        (b) Engraved by P. Maguire (fl. 1800–15); n.d.

        (c) Painted by John Barry (fl. 1784–1827); n.d. Reproduced with permission of the Trustees of Wesley's Chapel, City Road.

59   Anonymous engraver (after Barry); n.d.

60   (a) Painting attributed to Benjamin West, R.A. (1738–1820); n.d., Permission of the World Methodist Museum, Lake Junaluska.

        (b) Copy of Barry portrait; n.d. By permission of the Rector and Fellows of Lincoln College, Oxford.

62 Robert Hancock (1730–1817); 1790 (after J. Miller painting).

64 John Kay (1742–1826); 1790 (his drawing of three gentlemen walking in Edinburgh—Wesley in the middle).

65 (a) Silhouette by John Butterworth, Jr. (c. 1760–1820); 1790.

    (b) Small portrait by John Kay, 1790.

66 William Ridley (1764–1838); 1791 (Wesley lying in state at City Road Chapel).

67 Death mask, taken from Wesley, after March 2, 1791.

68 Anonymous, "John Wesley Carried by Angels into Abraham's Bosom" colored engraving, published on Aug. 1, 1791, by Robert Sayer.

69 Anonymous, biscuit cover from Wesley's funeral; March 9, 1791 (depicting Wesley's portrait, from Arnold).

70 William Bromley, A.R.A. (1769–1842); April 1791 (*European Magazine* portrait).

71 Two engravings by Thomas Holloway, R.A. (1748–1827):

    (a) Used as the frontispiece to volume one of John Hampson's biography of Wesley; Apr. 25, 1791.

    (b) Published by Holloway and R. Wilkinson; May 24, 1791.

72 (a) Engraved by N. Nasmyth; published by R. Grant in November 1791.

    (b) Engraved by William Greatbach; n.d. (used as frontispiece in 1851); original drawing attributed to Thomas Worlidge (1700–66).

    (c) Engraved by John Jones (1755–97); 1791 (after a 1784 painting by Louis Vaslet, fl. 1770–91).

    (d) Engraved by Thomas A. Dean (fl. 1835–59); 1836 (after Vaslet).

73 Delineated and engraved by J. Tookey (fl. 1785–1810); pub. Apr. 2, 1791.

74 Engraved by William Thomas Fry (1789–1843); 1824.

75 (a) Stipple engraving similar to Barry, originally by Charles Goodman (d. 1835) and Robert Piggott, re-published by William Smith, Philadelphia; c. 1830s. Bridwell Library Special Collections, Perkins School of Theology, Southern Methodist University.

    (b) Copper plate from which engraving was struck. Bridwell Library Special Collections, Perkins School of Theology, Southern Methodist University.

76   (a) Engraved by J[ohn] Palin; n.d. (profile after Edridge).

(b) Anonymous engraving, "Aristocratic" portrait; n.d.

77   (a) Anonymous, medallion; n.d., (after Williams).

(b) Anonymous, medallion, n.d. (after Zoffany, elements reversed).

(c) Anonymous, Seal of the Methodist Church in Great Britain, (after Flaxman and "Roubiliac" bust).

78   (a) Engraved by William Ridley (1764–1838), after Henry Edridge, A.R.A (1768–1821); 1790; frontispiece to Thomas Coke and Henry Moore, *The Life of the Rev. John Wesley, A.M.* (London, 1792).

(b) Engraved by R. Page (fl. 1813–23), copy of Edridge (reversed): 1829.

79   Later woodcut after Edridge, frontispiece in American Methodist hymnal, *A Collection of Hymns* (New York, 1843).

80   (a) Anonymous painted portrait of schoolboy, at John Street United Methodist Church, New York City; n.d. Courtesy of John Street United Methodist Church, New York, NY.

(b) Chalk drawing by John Downman (1750–1854) of an anonymous clergy; label on back says "Portrait of a Divine Called Reverend John Wesley," c. 1781. Courtesy of the Yale Center for British Art, Paul Mellon Collection.

(c) Advertised as painted portrait of John Wesley, n.d.; purchased by Frank Baker and given to the Rubenstein Library, Duke University.

(d) John Cennick, engraved by Philip Dawe (c. 1745–c. 1809), 1785 (after A. L. Brandt). © National Portrait Gallery, London.

(e) Anonymous painted portrait claimed as being by George Romney of John Wesley, at Wesley House, Cambridge, England; n.d.

82   Anonymous ivory bas-relief of unknown person; n.d. Bridwell Library Special Collections, Perkins School of Theology, Southern Methodist University, Dallas, TX.

85   John Jackson, R.A. (1778–1831); 1827. Reproduced with permission of the Trustees of Wesley's Chapel, City Road.

86   (a) Engraved by Thomas A. Dean (fl. 1835–59); 1850 (after John Jackson).

(b) Detail of Louis Glück micro-calligraphic drawing. Bridwell Library Special Collections, Perkins School of Theology, Southern Methodist University, Dallas, TX.

87   Script drawing by Louis Glück (1804–74, sometimes called

Rosenthal); c.1857. Bridwell Library Special Collections, Perkins School of Theology, Southern Methodist University, Dallas, TX.

88 William Hogarth (1697–1764). 1764 ("William Hogarth Painting the Comic Muse"); self portrait.

89 David Ryckaert III (1612–61), "Painter's Studio," 1638.

90 John Raphael Smith (1751–1812), 1773 ("Mrs. Macaroni and Her Gallant at a Print Shop"); printed for John Bowles, published Apr. 2, 1773.

91 Anonymous, engraver working at desk.

92 Paper pattern/design (backward image) for engraving on copperplate. John Price, Antiquarian Books (catalog), "Recent Acquisitions," July 2013.

93 Stradanus, sculpt., c. 1585 (sixteenth-century cheese-roller press for printing engraving).

94 Inscriptions on three different engravings of Hone's portrait of Wesley:

(a) Printed for Robert Sayer, Dec. 20, 1770.

(b) Printed for Carington Bowles, Dec. 3, 1770.

(c) Printed for Carington Bowles II and Samuel Carver, 1790s.

95 "Academicians of the Royal Academy," Johann Zoffany, 1772.

96 (a) Detail of Hunter, 1765.

(b) Detail of Hamilton, 1787.

(c) Detail of Romney, 1789.

(d) Detail of Arnold, 1790.

97 (a) Detail of anonymous portrait after Bone, 1782.

(b) Detail of Ranmoor, 1785.

(c) Detail of Tookey, 1791.

(d) Detail of Miller, 1790.

100 Enoch Wood (1759–1840), c. 1782 (bust of Wesley).

101 Bodlidge engraving of Wesley for volume one of the *Arminian Magazine*, 1778.

Selected Bibliography

Arminian Magazine 1, 2, 4 (1778, 1779, 1783).

Baker, Frank, "Papers [Collection of Portraits of John Wesley]." Durham, NC: Rubenstein Rare Book Library, 1930–2008.

Beck, Hilary. *Victorian Engravings.* London: Victoria and Albert Museum, 1973.

Bindman, David, ed. *The History of British Art: 1600–1970.* London and New Haven: Yale University Press for the Yale Center for British Art and Tate Museum, 2008.

Brash, W. B. "John Russell, R.A." WHS *Proceedings* 25 (1923, Part 2).

Chamberlain, Arthur B. *Thomas Gainsborough.* London: Duckworth, 1903.

Clayton, Timothy. *The English Print: 1688–1802.* London and New Haven: Yale University Press for the Yale Center for British Art, 1997.

Combe, William. *The Fanatic Saints: or, Bedlamites Inspired.* London, J. Bew, 1778.

_____. *Fanatical Conversion; or, Methodism Displayed.* London: J. Bew, 1779.

Curnock, Nehemiah, ed. *The Journal of the Rev. John Wesley, A.M.* London: Epworth Press, 1913–1938. 8 vols.

Cross, D. A. *A Striking Likeness: The Life of George Romney.* Aldershot: Ashgate, 2000.

Forsaith, Peter S. "Every Picture Tells a Story." *Wesley's Chapel Leysian Centre Magazine* 9 (Winter 1997/98).

_____. "John Wesley (1703–1791): An Outline Iconographic Survey [of artistic representations in Bridwell Library, Dallas, TX]." Private paper, 2002.

_____. "Material and Cultural Aspects of Methodism: Architecture, Artifacts and Art," in William Gibson, Peter Forsaith, and Martin Wellings, eds., *The Ashgate Research Companion to World Methodism*. Burlington: Ashgate, 2013.

_____. "Methodism and Its Images," in Charles Yrigoyen Jr., ed., *Companion to Methodism*. London: T & T Clark, 2010.

_____. "The Romney Portrait of John Wesley." *Methodist History* 47 (Part 4, July 2004).

Heitzenrater, Richard. *The Elusive Mr. Wesley*. 2nd ed. Nashville: Abingdon Press, 2003.

_____. "John Wesley's Early Sermons." *WHS Proceedings* 37 (Feb. 1970).

Kay, John. *Series of Original Portraits and Caricature Etchings by the Late John Kay, Miniature Painter*. Edinburgh: Paton, Carver, and Gilder, 1837.

Kerslake, John. *Early Georgian Portraits*. London: Her Majesty's Stationery Office, 1977. 2 vols.

Lister, Raymond. *Prints and Printmaking: A Dictionary and Handbook of the Art in Nineteenth-Century Britain*. London: Methuen, 1984.

Lloyd, Gareth. "John Wesley Images Collection [in the John Rylands University Library, Manchester, England]." Private paper, 2004.

Lloyd, Stephen, and Kim Sloan. *The Intimate Portrait: Drawings, Miniatures, and Pastels from Ramsay to Lawrence*. Edinburgh: National Galleries of Scotland; London: The British Museum, 2008.

Notes & Queries (3rd series) 7 (April 1, 1865).

O'Donoghue, Freeman M., and Henry Mendelssohn Hake. *Catalogue of Engraved British Portraits in the Department of Prints and Drawings in the British Museum*. Vols. IV (S–Z) and VI (Supplement). London: British Museum, 1908–25. 6 vols.

Penny, Nicholas, ed. *Reynolds*. New York: Abrams, 1986.

Pointon, Marcia. *Hanging the Head: Portraiture and Social Formation in Eighteenth-Century England*. New Haven: Yale University Press, 1993.

Rogal, Samuel J. *The Historical, Biographical, and Artistic Background of Extant Portrait Paintings and Engravings of John Wesley (1742–1951)*. Lewiston, NY: Edwin Mellen Press, 2003.

Ryan, Donald. "The Edinburgh Wesley Portraits." WHS *Proceedings* 55 (February 2005), 1–13.

_____. "The Micro-calligraphic portrait of John Wesley," WHS *Proceedings* 59 (Part 4, Feb. 2014): 136–48.

Smith, Mrs. Richard. *Mrs. Adam Clarke: Her Character and Correspondence, by Her Daughter*. London: Partridge & Oakey, 1851. Cited in Page A. Thomas, "John Wesley: Spiritual Advisor to Young Women as He Speaks through His Letters," Wesley Center Online, http://wesley.nnu.edu/?id=4723.

Taylor, Isaac. *Wesley and Methodism*. London: Longmans, 1851.

Telford, John. *Sayings and Portraits of John Wesley*. London: Epworth Press, 1924.

Tey, Josephine. *The Daughter of Time*. New York: Collier Books, 1988.

Walpole, Horace. *Anecdotes of Painting in England, 1760–1795, with Some Account of the Principal Artists*. 3 vols. London: Chatto and Windus, 1876.

_____. *A Catalogue of Engravers, who have been Born, or Resided in England, digested by Horace Walpole, Earl of Oxford, From the Mss. of Mr. George Vertue*. London: Caulfield, Coram, and Barrett, 1794.

Walter, Frank Keller. *Abbreviations and Technical Terms Used in Book Catalogs*. Boston: Faxon, 1919.

Webster, LaVere. *Many Faces: John Wesley*. Birmingham, MI: First Methodist Church, 2013.

Wesley, John. *The Works of John Wesley*. Bicentennial Edition. Oxford and Nashville: Oxford University Press and Abingdon Press, 1976–. 17 vols. printed of projected 34 vols.

Wright, Joseph G. "Wesley Portraits." WHS *Proceedings* 2 (Part 3, 1899); 3 (Part 7, 1902); 4 (Part 1, 1903).

General Index

120

www.ingramcontent.com/pod-product-compliance
Lightning Source LLC
Chambersburg PA
CBHW080423190526
45161CB00004B/261